Women for the Harvest

Peggy Shirley

Cover design by: Jeremy Shirley

2010

Dedication

To my best friend, Jesus Christ, who actually wrote this book. I owe Him all the glory for giving me the words to write. It truly is His book that I pray He will use to encourage women all around the world to fulfill their God-given destinies. This book would not have been written without the relentless and persistent encouragement from my amazing husband Delron and son Jeremy. God only knows the hours, patience, and perseverance that it took from my devoted husband to edit and retype this book. I am forever grateful.

Carol and Konya, your hours of editing and typing this book along with your encouragement are so appreciated and made this book a reality.

Table of Contents

INTRODUCTION

As I lay in my bed in Pokhara, Nepal, growing closer and closer to unconsciousness -- all the while, shaking uncontrollably with chills, yet burning up with a fever -- I wondered if this was how my life was to end. I had just begun to participate in the Great Commission as a short-term missionary. I had finally begun to see in II Corinthians 4:3-4:

> And even if our gospel is veiled, it is veiled to those who are perishing, in whose case the god of this world has blinded the minds of the unbelieving so that they might not see the light of the gospel of the glory of Christ, who is the image of God. (NAS)

However, when I spoke the truth of the Word of God, blinders came off the non-believers and the truth of the Good News was setting people free. The Buddhists and Hindus were just waiting to hear the news about Jesus Christ. They were eager to respond when they heard that He was what they had been searching for. What joy and excitement I experienced when I saw God reveal Himself to these lost souls. I was thrilled to witness the resulting happiness in them when they became new converts.

My husband and I, along with our mission team, had been preaching for several days in Nepal, a primarily Hindu nation which had recently opened their doors to the gospel. Before this time, we could have been imprisoned for preaching in Jesus' name. Now we carefully began holding meetings and watched in amazement as God saved, healed,

1

delivered, and did the miraculous. I was just beginning to relax and realize that it was His hand upon mine and His anointing on my words that made these things possible. The Lord had brought me such a long way from when I was first saved. Back then the thought of doing mission work had never entered my mind; I was still uncomfortable witnessing and laying hands on the sick in my own town, much less going to the ends of the earth to share my faith! But then Romans 10:13-14 jumped off the page at me:

> For whosoever shall call upon the name of the Lord shall be saved. How then shall they call on him in whom they have not believed? And how shall they believe in him of whom they have not heard? and how shall they hear without a preacher?

The challenge of these words had finally brought me to become a woman for the harvest. But now I lay in what I thought to be a deathbed. Why had He brought me so far for my ministry to end so abruptly?

My husband and the rest of the team had gone on to hold a meeting, not realizing how sick I was. Mustering all my energy, in a whisper, I asked the one team member who stayed back with me what the awful stench was that was coming into our room. She looked out the window, upset as she reported that our room was directly above a statue of King Cobra, one of the gods the Hindus worship. She answered that the odor was coming from the incense they were offering to this statue. She went on to say that the devotees were offering food and ringing bells, inviting demonic spirits. Just what I needed to hear! I asked her to please start singing Oh, the Blood of Jesus and to believe God for a miracle. I felt like I was dying as depressing and desperate imaginations such as the thoughts that I would never see my children and husband again raced through my mind. "Lord," I cried, "did you send me here to die? I have too much work to do for you, and my kids will not have a mother." As my friend paced the floor singing and praying, we heard a knock on the door. Who could it possibly be? All the people we knew were at the meeting. Again another knock. Little did we know that on the other side of the door was one of God's messengers. When Angie opened the door, she was greeted by a polite Nepali man with a doctor's bag. As he gently entered the room, he spoke to us in perfect English and told me that I was a very sick woman. He then added that I would soon be just fine. I kept thinking to myself, "How did he find me? Who sent him?" There is only one doctor for every 25,000 people in Nepal. When we passed by health clinics, we would see long lines of people waiting and were told how they had to wait for hours to see a doctor. And now here was a kind doctor who actually came to me. He checked me over, gave my friend some instructions, left some medicine, and seemed to leave as quickly as he had come. How relieved I felt! The Lord had heard our prayers. My companion kept saying, "Soon you will be fine, Peggy. You will be fine just as the doctor had told you." We prayed and thanked the Lord, and shortly after I was asleep. When I woke up, I was soaking wet with no sign of fever. Though I was still very weak, I knew that the worst was over and that my healing was surely starting to manifest.

At long last. my husband came back from the service and was shocked to see my condition. I told him what had happened and how thankful I was that he had somehow arranged for a doctor to visit me. He responded pensively, "Peggy, we did not send a doctor. We did not know how sick you were. Besides that, there are no doctors around here." I remembered telling Angie that our visitor must have been an angel, but I really thought that it had been my fever speaking to say such a thing. But now I was beginning to wonder if my musing might have really been the truth! We checked with our Nepali team leader and the hotel manager, but no one knew a thing about sending for a doctor. God knew my need and -- through His mercy, love, and faithfulness -- sent just what I needed. He could have healed me without sending a doctor, but it was even more exciting and awesome for me to see how God sent an angel from nowhere to bring my healing. The next day my sickness was over. Though tired and weak, I was able to finish our trip and was soon totally restored, healed, and back to the work God had for me to do.

I believe that He has much work for those of you reading this book. Although I have been in the ministry for many years now, I never tire of telling others how ripe the harvest is. The world is full of people waiting to receive prayer and the gospel --not only on the mission field, but also in the United States. The problem remains that there are never enough laborers, especially women, in the harvest fields.

The material in this book has been birthed out of my experience as a woman who, for lack of proper knowledge, was spiritually perishing just as realistically as I was physically perishing in that dingy hotel room in the Himalayan kingdom of Nepal. For many years, I sat in the church pew watching the men do it all. I had been taught, "Sister Peggy, you must listen to the Word of God that says women are to be silent in the church. You are never to teach men or be in leadership positions. You are to be under the men who are over you in the Lord at all times." This negative teaching was sucking the spiritual life out of me just as certainly as the raging fever had tried to suck out my physical life.

Then God began to cause a stirring in my heart. How could I not do something for Him after all He had done for me? How could I not teach and do what I saw the men do when the Word, over and over, commanded me to be involved in the Great Commission? The Lord began to renew my mind, showing me that I, a woman, was created in His image.

> And God said, Let us make man in our image, after our likeness: and let them have dominion over the fish of the sea, and over the fowl of the air, and over the cattle, and over all the earth, and over every creeping thing that creepeth upon the earth. So God created man in his own image, in the image of God created he him; male and female created he them. (Genesis 1:26-27)

5

I learned that I was equal to man and had been given co-dominion with him. As I studied more and more of God's Word, I began to shake off the false teaching I had been given and was set free to become the woman of the harvest that God called me to be.

Just as the Lord sent an angelic doctor into my room with the right medicine, He began to send teachers with the proper interpretation of the scriptures to bring as radical a healing to my spirit as the doctor's treatment brought to my body. Along with this, God picked just the right husband for me, who, unlike other Christian men, began stirring up the gifts in me and teaching me scriptures in their proper context -- scriptures that had been used to keep women from coming into their rightful place beside the men -- working together as co-laborers for the Lord. Together we studied the great women in the Bible who did noteworthy exploits for the Lord. I found that Paul commended not just the sweet "Mary"s and "Martha"s, but I also began to learn about women whom I had never heard of: bold women like Junia, an apostle; Phoebe, an evangelist; Priscilla, a teacher and pastor; and others whom God used in the five-fold ministry.

The next part of my journey into becoming the servant of God He had called me to be was for me to do a "housecleaning" -- not in my home, but inside myself. Oh, it was not easy; in fact, many times it was such a painful job that I wanted to run away rather than go through it. There were many things that God was dealing with inside of me -- things that I just wanted to "sweep under the rug." But He was insistent because He was cleaning and purifying me for His service.

As I realized the issues, such as the "fear of man," which held me in bondage, God gently began to do the work of setting me free. He showed me over and over that He doesn't need "perfect" vessels. If He did, He would have no servants at all. He is just looking for "purified" vessels. That is why all Christians need to go through a continual process of housecleaning if we are to stay clean and ready for His service.

> If a man therefore purge himself from these, he shall be a vessel unto honour, sanctified, and meet for the master's use, and prepared unto every good work. (II Timothy 2:21)

The Lord then began to bring well-known women Christian leaders into my life. They began to mentor me and teach me the "do"s and "don't"s of being a "lady" in ministry. I spent hours watching, listening, and asking all sorts of woman-to-woman questions. Whereas I had only read and been taught about all the great men in the Bible and their stories, now God was letting me see firsthand the anointing and call on women -- women who, although they had become national leaders, were simply women just like me. I truly got the revelation of Galatians 3:28, that in God's eyes, there is no male nor female for we are all one in Christ Jesus. To the Lord, we are all the same.

He is looking for vessels to pour "into" and "out of" -- vessels who will say to the Lord, not "Who am I?" but "Here am I!" I could write volumes on what the Lord has done to me and through me as a woman who dared to step out in trust and to obey God to do whatever He put before me. It has been over thirty years for me now: being a woman for the harvest, doing things I never would have thought that this once-fearful woman could do and going places that I would never have dreamed of, even in my wildest fantasies. Now I know that God always wanted me to be a laborer in the army of God. I am convinced that this misunderstanding and false teaching that women aren't called as well as men is the greatest lie ever told -- and believed.

There is no greater joy or satisfaction that we will ever find in this world than preaching, healing, delivering, or teaching people about Him. James 4:14 says, "Yet you do not know what your life will be like tomorrow. You are just a vapor that appears for a little while and then vanishes away." (NAS) What we do for Him on this earth counts forever in eternity.

My hope and desire as you read these lessons is that each of you will individually find yourself in one of three groups. If you are in group number one who have never done much for the Lord, my hope is that a flame (or passion) be ignited. For those of you in group number two who are already serving the Lord but might have been hurt or discouraged and have, therefore, started to let your flame start to wane, my hope is that this book will fan or rekindle your flame. For those in group number three whose flames are lit, my hope is that reading this material will take your flame up to another level and that He will continue to stretch and expand you for even greater works so that He may be glorified. Regardless of which category you find yourself in, my prayer is that this book will inspire you to say the following prayer along with me:

"Lord, if You can use anybody, then here I am. Open the doors. Lead me to people and places that only You can do. Thank You for the courage and Your precious anointing and presence and let me bring glory to Your name."

Chapter One

YOUR DESIRE IS FROM YOUR DESIGNER

The reason you have a desire to be a woman for the harvest is something God -- not man -- has placed inside of you. It is His job (with your permission) to fulfill it. It is also scriptural. First Corinthians 14:1 tells us "EAGERLY PURSUE and seek to acquire [this] love [make it your aim, your great quest]; and earnestly desire and cultivate the spiritual endowments (gifts), especially that you may prophesy (interpret the divine will and purpose in inspired preaching and teaching)." (AMP) and I Timothy 4:14 says, "Do not neglect the gift which is in you, [that special inward endowment] which was directly imparted to you [by the Holy Spirit] by prophetic utterance when the elders laid their hands upon you [at your ordination]." (AMP)

In the story of the talents in Matthew 25:14-15, all the servants were given at least one talent. It is our job to let the Lord show us what our gifts are and to give Him permission to develop these gifts and talents in us. Some will be given more talents than others; thus, they will have more responsibility. For some, their calling will be to travel to foreign countries and hold huge meetings; for others, their ministry will be in small settings such as cell groups or simply one-on-one. Both are equally important and needed for His kingdom's purposes.

What can you do? The answer is simple: anything God has called you to do! Many women think that because they have been given limited, if any, roles in the church that they are of no value.

However, there is much work that the Lord will open up for them outside the church -- tasks and responsibilities that will prove that these women truly are treasures, even if they are not recognized as such in the church.

We will study women in the Bible, as well as women of recent history, who listened to their spirits and received their assignments from God even though men gave them nothing to do.

God isn't interested in your excuses -- only your results. He is looking for your availability -- not your ability. I can guarantee you that you won't be totally fulfilled as a woman until you are serving Him in some way. First Corinthians 1:24-31 says:

> But to those who are called, whether Jew or Greek (Gentile), Christ [is] the Power of God and the Wisdom of God. [This is] because the foolish thing [that has its source in] God is wiser than men, and the weak thing [that springs] from God is stronger than men. For [simply] consider your own call, brethren; not many [of you were considered to be] wise according to human estimates and standards, not many influential and powerful, not many of high and noble birth. [No] for God selected (deliberately chose) what in the world is foolish to put the wise to shame, and what the world calls weak to put the strong to shame. And God also selected (deliberately chose) what in the world is lowborn

and insignificant and branded and treated with contempt, even the things that are nothing, that He might depose and bring to nothing the things that are, So that no mortal man should [have pretense for glorying and] boast in the presence of God. But it is from Him that you have your life in Christ Jesus, Whom God made our Wisdom from God, [revealed to us a knowledge of the divine plan of salvation previously hidden, manifesting itself as] our Righteousness [thus making us upright and putting us in right standing with God], and our Consecration [making us pure and holy], and our Redemption [providing our ransom from eternal penalty for sin]. So then, as it is written, Let him who boasts and proudly rejoices and glories, boast and proudly rejoice and glory in the Lord. (AMP)

I have chosen to write this material because I have seen church after church in nation after nation that did not realize the tremendous treasure that women are to the Body. I want to wake up, shake up, and stir up the call that is on your life as a woman.

Women are coming into their place -- not below the men, not above the men, not behind the men -- but beside the men. We compliment and complete the men in the Body of Christ. This call to take their place beside the men is happening around the world. When I met an apostle who was over many churches in Africa, I told him what the Lord had showed me about women being great assets to the churches. He was reluctant to allow the women in his church to do any five-fold ministry or use their gifts. I then asked him if he would take the time upon his return to Africa to ask the Lord what He thought about women. A year later, he visited the States again and asked to meet with me. Humbly he said how he took my advice and the Lord spoke these words to him, "The reason your churches are so barren is because your women are being kept barren. Women were created to give not only physical birth, but spiritual birth as well." He then began to teach, release, and even ordain the women in all the churches he oversaw. With time, he began to experience noticeable growth with much fruit. The growth was noteworthy enough that other pastors of different churches began to ask him what he was doing differently. He answered simply, "Tap into the hidden treasure you have -- your women!"

For a family to be "functional," it needs both a father and a mother. It is no different in the church family. Women's spiritual gifts, guidance, leadership, and works are needed and necessary to help the church meet all the needs of the people and keep the church from becoming dysfunctional. It is time to get back to the truths of Acts 2:17-18:

> And it shall come to pass in the last
> days, saith God, I will pour out of my
> Spirit upon all flesh: and your sons
> and your daughters shall prophesy,
> and your young men shall see

visions, and your old men shall
dream dreams: And on my servants
and on my handmaidens I will pour
out in those days of my Spirit; and
they shall prophesy.

These are the last days, and women are being
stirred up and called to minister around the world.
It is the Holy Spirit calling "deep to deep!"

Four Barriers That Have Kept Women Barren

There are many reasons why women have been
kept back from fulfilling their call or using their gifts
for the Lord. I have chosen the following as those
from which most other obstacles flow.

1) Satan

Right from the beginning, Satan was out to stop
women. Not only did he deceive Eve into eating the
forbidden fruit, he soon discovered that his ultimate
undoing was to come through the seed of the
woman:

And the LORD God said unto the
serpent, Because thou hast done
this, thou art cursed above all cattle,
and above every beast of the field;
upon thy belly shalt thou go, and
dust shalt thou eat all the days of
thy life: And I will put enmity
between thee and the woman, and
between thy seed and her seed; it
shall bruise thy head, and thou shalt
bruise his heel. (Genesis 3:14-15)

He hates women and is very aware of the
powerful potential they have in stopping his work.
He knows that women complete the army of God

14

against him. He also knows that women were created uniquely and different from men to accomplish much for the Lord's kingdom. God created both Adam and Eve for His purposes and when they work together, there is nothing that can't be accomplished!

2) <u>Lack</u> <u>of</u> <u>Knowledge</u>

As I travel around the world and see how Christian women are being treated, especially knowing what the Word of God says about women, it is very disheartening. Hosea 4:6 says that people -- and that includes women -- "are destroyed for lack of knowledge." Women need to get a revelation of how special they are, how much God loves them, and how He desires for them to be part of His work upon the earth. My life was changed when I discovered the real truths about what Jesus thought about women. "And you shall know the truth and the truth shall set you free." (John 8:32, AMP) There have been many scriptures which are subject to misinterpretation, but the misunderstanding of I Corinthians 14:34-35 and I Timothy 2:11-15 have been especially harmful to women. These two passages of scripture are used to defend the notion that women cannot teach or preach. We will be studying these scriptures in their proper context later in the book and will discover their correct interpretation. In addition, we will examine many other scriptures where Paul talks about women who co-labored with him in the gospel.

There are many women in the Bible such as Junia, Typhenia, and Typhora, whom most Christian women don't even know about even though they were noted by Paul as his co-laborers in the gospel.

Some even functioned in the five-fold ministry.

Certainly, women were treated as third-class citizens in Bible days -- a dishonor which continues even today in some churches and countries. However, we will study a list of special distinctions that Jesus gave to women to show that God thinks women are not inferior to men and that they can be called into spiritual service just as well as men.

3) Fear and Low Self-esteem

These two characteristics are very common in women and are greatly magnified by Satan. A little acrostic based on the word "fear" can help us get a grasp on exactly what it is that the enemy is up to: False Evidence Appearing Real. Satan tries to convince women that they do not have what it takes to accomplish anything for the Lord. Women need to be set free from a poor self-image and the negative things said or done to them in the past. Otherwise, Satan will use these negatives to stop them. If the Lord doesn't care about your age, education, or natural abilities, why should you? God says to us, "I didn't call you because you could; I called you because you would." Proverbs 29:25 tells us that "The fear of man brings a snare, but whoever leans on, trusts in, and puts his confidence in the Lord is safe and set on high." (AMP) Psalms 34:4 reassures us that "I sought (inquired of) the Lord and required Him [of necessity and on the authority of His Word], and He heard me, and delivered me from all my fears." (AMP)

Because there is a serious lack of women mentors and leaders in the church to encourage and teach other women what and what not to do, fear and low self-esteem have run rampant through the

Body of Christ. I believe that a major part of my calling is to combat this malady in the women of the church today. I know what it is like to have wasted years because I had no one to help me break free from these bondages. If only I would have had a godly woman mentor to share with me the information I am giving you in this book, my life would have been radically different. Because I lacked the liberating truth, it took me years of experience to realize what I am going to share with you here. It is my prayer that these truths liberate you and set you free from fear and low self-esteem so that you can be the woman of God that you have been called to be.

4) <u>Men</u> <u>and</u> <u>Denominational</u> <u>Doctrines</u>

Through the years, men and denominational doctrines have denied or greatly restricted women in the work that they wanted to do for the Lord. Many men have been mistakenly taught that women are to be silent and inactive in church -- except for possibly teaching other women and children. Therefore, they would never think of considering a woman for any of the five-fold giftings. Marilyn Hickey's husband Wallace said that instead of getting into a lengthy explanation of why he thinks that women should be able to preach, he simply states, "You know, when I look around and see the world dying and going to hell, I really don't believe God cares very much who brings the saving message." A truly secure man has no problem with women in the ministry; instead, he welcomes them to co-labor together for Christ to get the job done! Remember, women, man did not give you your gifts and calling, so even if man tries to suppress them, he cannot take them away.   "For God's gifts and His call are irrevocable. [He never withdraws them when once they are given, and He does not change His mind about those to whom He gives His grace or to whom He sends His call.]" (Romans 11:29, AMP)   In other words, He won't take back the gifts He has given to you.

A woman was created for a purpose -- different from man for a reason:

Warriors and winners

One of a kind (unique)

Made to serve Him as a handmaiden of the Lord

Anointed

Needed -- The harvest is plentiful, but the laborers are few.

Chapter Two

PRIDE AND PREJUDICE

Recently I watched the movie, Pride and Prejudice, again and was struck by all the sadness and heartache the sisters had to face simply because they were women with inferior positions in society. How I applauded Elizabeth when she stood up for herself and boldly told Mr. Darcy that he was full of pride and prejudice towards women and insisted that such an attitude was tragically wrong. Because of the truth she confidently exposed, Mr. Darcy's eyes were opened and his attitude change brought the movie to a happy ending.

The movie Becoming Jane depicts how Jane Austin, who would one day be heralded as a famous classic writer could barely get people to acknowledge her writings. The rejection was not because hers was not excellent reading material, but simply because the material was written by a woman. That was not "acceptable." She, too, was faced with pride and prejudice because of her gender and position in society. Women have not had it easy throughout history; and, as we all know, have not been treated equal to men since the beginning of time. Sad to say, this is still true, especially in many foreign countries.

I will never forget how, on one of my mission trips, as we all gathered to sit down at the table of the home of a Christian pastor, I was told, "You will have to eat in the kitchen with the other women." My husband overheard this remark and proceeded to boldly pull out a chair for me at the table with all the men to let them know his position. This reminded me of how the women in biblical times were treated. Just as Jesus came and openly showed the men that He did not approve of the Jewish laws they wrote about women, so had my dear husband let the men know that women, as well as the men, should sit together at the table. It wasn't the most enjoyable meal of my life; but, over time, my husband and I were able to teach these friends, as well as hundreds of other men and women around the world, about the equality of men and women which God had established in Genesis.

Certainly any type of pride or prejudice towards women, yesterday or today, is not from God. When I began developing the Women for the Harvest course which I have taught in Bible college settings and in seminars across the country and around the world, not only did I have trouble finding women in ministry from history, but I also found a shortage of women in the Bible who had ministered. Why weren't there more women such as Aimee Semple McPherson or Kathryn Kuhlman? Where were they? Why weren't there more women ministers in the Bible? Yes, we had Deborah, a great judge over the land, and others, but why couldn't I find more women? As I began to research and ask older Christians, it came down to the two scriptures taken out of context which I have mentioned before -- I Corinthians 14:34-35 and I Timothy 2:11-12.

From the beginning, women of the United States were told that they could not teach or preach but that they could go as missionaries outside of the United States and freely minister. Consequently, you will find wonderful stories about women missionaries, such as Lillian Trasher, Amy Carmichael, and so many more, and read about the signs and wonders they did in foreign countries. What foolish thinking! Why would Jesus allow and anoint women to minister to His children in one country but not another? If He didn't want them to teach or be used, He would have made it clear. But instead man, because of his prejudice and ignorance and misunderstanding of the scriptures -- not the Lord -- has stopped women. Women, too, have believed this misunderstanding of the scriptures. Yet one basic question remains -- why did He put the desire in women to work in the ministry if He wouldn't fulfill it? I wanted to just hide beside my husband and stay comfortable in my pew in church, but God kept after me until I had no choice but to say, "Here I am, Lord. Send me." Why does this debate still go on when there is clearly a shortage of laborers and thousands are dying and going to hell?

I am reminded of the pastor in Sri Lanka who told me that he was exhausted because he was over five churches. Yet he wouldn't let his women serve in the ministry because of what he thought the Bible said. I wonder how many victories the devil, our adversary, must have won in that city because the pastor was trying to do all the work single-handedly. But this exclusiveness is slowly changing and the pride and the prejudice against women preachers are gradually being erased. The truth is coming forth and the women are being set free to go out into the harvest fields to set many more free.

Let's go back to biblical times and see where all this pride and prejudice came from. Moses wrote the first five books of the Bible which was the Jewish

21

law, called the Torah. The Talmud, the Jewish interpretation of the Torah, contains the rules the Jewish men made about women. This is also referred to as their "law." These rules were not what God gave them; they were their own beliefs. Let's look at the Jewish attitude toward women in biblical times. Charles Tromley wrote in his book, Who Said Women Can't Teach?, that the Jewish men prayed a daily thanksgiving prayer that went like this: "Praise be to God that He has not created me a Gentile; praise be to God that He has not created me a woman; praise be to God that he has not created me an ignorant man." One of the greatest insults was to call a Jewish man a gentile, a slave, or a fool. These three groups of humans had the lowest status possible. By equalizing women with them, the men revealed what was in their hearts. They thanked God daily for not being a woman. This prayer is still prayed by ultra-orthodox Jews. Josephus, a well-known Jewish historian wrote, "The woman is in all things inferior to the man. Let her accordingly be submissive." A man could divorce his wife at will, but under no circumstance could a wife divorce her husband. Only men spoke in public. No woman could give a testimony or conduct business. Generally, the attitude toward women was one of disregard, subjugation, and repression. Jewish women were to be seen as little as possible and heard even less. Throughout the Talmud, the rabbis constantly blamed sin, death, and suffering on Eve. This blame gave them reason to debase women. Only the rabbis knew the Hebrew language and the law of Moses, and they refused to teach women. As a result, few were learned. Since women weren't being educated in the Torah or expected to fulfill it, they were valueless to Judaism.

Some of you may remember the movie Yentel in which Barbara Streisand was cast as a Jewish girl who had to dress and act like a Jewish boy so she could go to school and learn the Torah and Talmud. Jewish women never asked their husbands questions in public. They sat fifteen steps below the men in a separate court. A woman was human property. A man could even sell his daughters. Even when the Roman, Egyptian, and Hellenistic cultures abandoned the ancient tribal practices of subjugating women, the Jews stuck to their tribal customs. Worse yet -- even when they accepted Christ, they kept the Jewish laws and customs. When I Corinthians 14:34 says, "Let your women keep silent...as also saith the law," Paul was referring to the Jewish oral law which was made up of what the rabbis thought the Torah meant. So it was the Jewish law, not the Bible, that demanded the silence of women. That law was not the original, inspired word of God spoken through the mouth of holy men of God -- it was Jewish traditionalism.

Turning to secular history, let's look briefly at life in the United States. It wasn't until the 1900s that women were allowed into men's universities. I have a dear friend, in her 90s now, who had to struggle and push herself into the University of Notre Dame graduate program. She was totally qualified, but because she was a woman and not a man, she had to fight to be accepted. It wasn't until 1920 that women got the right to vote. When in 2008 we had a woman run for the vice-presidency, I thought, "We have truly come a long way, baby!" From not even having the right to vote to being able to contend for the second highest office of the land, women have been able to step to a wonderful level of freedom from pride and prejudice. If only this same freedom could follow in the church!

Unfortunately, in many denominations today in the United States as well as abroad, the women are still not considered equal to men and are very mistreated. Dr. David Yonggi Cho of South Korea, who pastors what was at one time the largest church in the world, tells the story of how he came to finally use the women in his church as associate pastors and cell group leaders who instruct women as well as men. His church was growing very rapidly, and with all this came a lot of work and stress. Soon his health began to decline. His mother-in-law kept telling him that it was time to start training and using the women to help with the church, but he said, "Never!" The oriental culture of South Korea decisively puts women in a subordinate role throughout the society. At first, it was very difficult for Dr. Cho to think of delegating authority to the women in his church. He thought that the men would rebel and that the whole church, as well as all of Korean society, would turn against him. Besides, didn't the scriptures themselves say women should keep silent in the churches? That is what Paul had written to Timothy in I Timothy 2:12. He could relate to that because in many Korean churches, it had been the custom to separate the men from the women in the worship services. A large curtain was strung down the center aisle so they could not even see one another. But some of the women would whisper through the curtains to their husbands and create a disturbance.

When Dr. Cho came to our former church in Indiana, I saw this male-female separation first-hand. The men walked ahead of the women. They, not the women, went first through any doors. When they sat for the service, the women sat on one side in the pews across the aisle from the men. Dr. Cho went on to say that when he was giving the Lord all his objections about how using women wouldn't work, the Lord distinctly answered him, "Cho, that's your idea. My idea is to use the women." Then Dr. Cho said, "Lord, if you really want me to use women, you'll have to prove it to me from scripture." As he began studying the scriptures, he found that Paul was really not a male chauvinist after all. He frequently used women in his ministry and let people know they were under his authority -- not usurping it. Dr. Cho believes that it is important for women to have a covering and protection.

Then the Lord began to speak to him and gave him this beautiful prophecy:

Yonggi Cho, from whom was I born?
From woman, Lord.
And on whose lap was I nurtured?
Woman's, Lord.
Who stayed until the last at the crucifixion?
Women.
Who came to anoint My body in the tomb?
Women.

Who was the first witness of the resurrection?

Mary Magdalene, a woman.

To all of the questions you have answered, "women." Then why are you afraid of women? During My earthly ministry, I was surrounded by dear wonderful women. So why shouldn't my Body, the church, be surrounded and supported by women as well?

Then Dr. Cho said, "What else could I do? The Lord had made it clear to me that it was His will to use the women in the church." When Dr. Cho spoke at our church in Indiana, he said, "Women are the greatest evangelistic tools of my church. Some day America and other countries will catch on!" Now the majority of his cell group leaders and associate pastors are women.

Even after more than thirty years in the ministry, I am still convinced that there will always be an element of pride and prejudice towards women, but I know whom I serve, who called me, and to whom I must one day give an account for my life and what I did for Him. "The harvest is indeed plentiful, but the laborers are few." (Matthew 9:37, AMP) I must be one of those laborers. So must you, regardless of who has a prideful prejudice against it!

Jesus Came to Set Captive Women Free

From this lesson we will see how Jesus openly showed His defiance of the ways the Jewish men treated the Jewish women during biblical times. Remember, Moses wrote the first five books of the

Bible, called the Torah, under the inspiration of the Holy Ghost. It was the Jewish rabbis who interpreted it, and from this biased, superior outlook towards women came the Jewish laws in the Talmud regarding what a woman could and could not do. In Genesis 1:26-27, God made it clear that women were not inferior in His sight when He said, "Let us make man in Our image, according to Our likeness; let "them" have dominion over...all the earth...So God created man in His own image; in the image of God He created him; male and female He created them." We were created equal to men. In the United States, women created the ERA (Equal Rights Amendment) movement in the 1970s which openly challenged job discrimination, lower pay for women than for men, and a list of other grievances women had. It did change a lot of unfair practices and accomplished some good things which helped women to be treated more fairly and equally. However, it became a radical feminist movement led by women who were angry and bitter. As Christian women, we see this movement as a counterfeit to what God intends to do or has already done for us. We are not feminists. We are women who believe in God and His Word. Through what He did on Calvary, we are already liberated women! Satan hates this restoration of women to where they should be in the Body of Christ. He knows women, as well as men, were always meant to co-labor together in the army of God. In fact, Paul mentions women in several scriptures who worked beside him in the ministry. A few are Euodia and Syntyche in Philippians 4:2-3 and Junia in Romans 16:7. We will examine these women and many others as we go through the rest of our study.

In her book, The Emerging Christian Woman, Anne Jimenez says that women are "God's secret weapon." She goes on to call them "an untapped resource of teachers, administrators, speakers and more." She adds, "Never has it been more important that women step forward and accept their place beside the men in the church."

Neither Anne Jimenez nor I would tell ladies to usurp authority as I Timothy 2:12 has warned against. It is only through prayer and the right attitude that the Lord will make ministry opportunities possible for us. There are already some churches which see men and women as a team. They see the need for input and ministry from both males and females with their unique qualities and characteristics. However, many churches do not have this revelation. Do what you can in your church, but remember, most of what you will be called to do may be outside the church.

Let us look at some things Jesus did publicly for and to the women -- things that were directly opposed to the Jewish law and traditions. In the following stories, we will see how He openly displayed a truly revolutionary attitude toward women in the sense that He was overthrowing the social practices of the day by treating the women with respect, honor, and dignity. In short, He treated them equal to men since He created them both equally in His image. Apparently, Jesus was out to show the men that the way they treated women by putting such binding restrictions on them was man's idea, not the Lord's.

Jesus openly taught women. As we have

already discussed, women at this time were not allowed to be taught. As one ancient rabbi put it, "A woman has no right to learning except in the use of the spindle." The Talmud actually condemns a father who dared to teach the Word of God to his daughters, saying, "Whoever teaches his daughter the Torah is as though he taught her obscenity." However, Luke 10:38-42 says:

> Now it came to pass, as they went, that he entered into a certain village: and a certain woman named Martha received him into her house. And she had a sister called Mary, which also sat at Jesus' feet, and heard his word. But Martha was cumbered about much serving, and came to him, and said, Lord, dost thou not care that my sister hath left me to serve alone? bid her therefore that she help me. And Jesus answered and said unto her, Martha, Martha, thou art careful and troubled about many things: But one thing is needful: and Mary hath chosen that good part, which shall not be taken away from her. (emphasis added)

Jesus took the time to teach Mary as she sat at His feet and learned freely from Him.

Jesus openly touched women. Jewish law said that women weren't allowed to be touched. A Jewish merchant would not even count money back into the hand of a woman lest he touch her and become contaminated. Jesus, on the other hand, openly touched a woman and ministered to her with

29

no regard for any of the cultural taboos of the time.

Now He was teaching in one of the synagogues on the Sabbath. And behold, there was a woman who had a spirit of infirmity eighteen years, and was bent over and could in no way raise herself up. But when Jesus saw her, He called her to Him and said to her, Woman, you are loosed from your infirmity. <u>And He laid His hands on her, and immediately she was made straight, and glorified God.</u> (Luke 13:10-13, emphasis added)

<u>He let women touch Him.</u>

And one of the Pharisees desired him that he would eat with him. And he went into the Pharisee's house, and sat down to meat. And, behold, <u>a woman</u> in the city, which was a sinner, when she knew that Jesus sat at meat in the Pharisee's house, brought an alabaster box of ointment, And stood at his feet behind him weeping, and <u>began to wash his feet with tears, and did wipe them with the hairs of her head, and kissed his feet, and anointed them with the ointment.</u> Now when the Pharisee which had bidden him saw it, he spake within himself, saying, This man, if he were a prophet, would have known who and what manner of woman this is

30

that toucheth him: for she is a sinner. And Jesus answering said unto him, Simon, I have somewhat to say unto thee. And he saith, Master, say on. There was a certain creditor which had two debtors: the one owed five hundred pence, and the other fifty. And when they had nothing to pay, he frankly forgave them both. Tell me therefore, which of them will love him most? Simon answered and said, I suppose that he, to whom he forgave most. And he said unto him, Thou hast rightly judged. And he turned to the woman, and said unto Simon, Seest thou this woman? I entered into thine house, thou gavest me no water for my feet: but she hath washed my feet with tears, and wiped them with the hairs of her head. Thou gavest me no kiss: but this woman since the time I came in hath not ceased to kiss my feet. My head with oil thou didst not anoint: but this woman hath anointed my feet with ointment. Wherefore I say unto thee, Her sins, which are many, are forgiven; for she loved much: but to whom little is forgiven, the same loveth little. And he said unto her, Thy sins are forgiven. And they that sat at meat with him began to

> say within themselves, Who is this
> that forgiveth sins also? And he
> said to the woman, Thy faith hath
> saved thee; go in peace. (Luke
> 7:36-50, emphasis added)
> Verily I say unto you, Wheresoever
> this gospel shall be preached in the
> whole world, there shall also this,
> that this woman hath done, be told
> for a memorial of her. (Matthew
> 26:13)

He openly spoke to a woman. Jesus' very public ministry to the Samaritan woman at the well contradicted the accepted practice for a Jewish male of His day. Jesus not only talked to a woman in public, but He also instructed her and revealed Himself to her as the Messiah. The story is told in John 4:4-42, but of special interest are verses twenty-seven and thirty-nine where we see that Jesus unashamedly carried on an in-depth discussion with this woman, surprising even His own disciples.

> And upon this came his disciples,
> and marvelled that he talked with
> the woman: yet no man said, What
> seekest thou? or, Why talkest thou
> with her? (verse 27)
> And many of the Samaritans of that
> city believed on him for the saying of
> the woman, which testified, He told
> me all that ever I did. (verse 39)

Not only did Jesus break the custom which forbad men to speak to women in public ,but He also spoke to a woman of the Samaritans who were despised by the Jews. She was also looked down upon by her fellow Samaritans because she had quite a past with all of her divorces and reputation with men. Jesus knew all of this and purposely chose her over others to show His unconditional love. Not only did He reveal Himself to her as the Messiah, but He used her, a woman, to bring salvation to many in her city.

Jesus came to give all women a second chance despite their pasts. In Matthew 1:3-16, which lists the genealogy of Jesus Christ, the evangelist chose to mention four women with pasts who, like the Samaritan woman, were despised because of their sins: Tamar, Rahab, Ruth, and Bathsheba. Among these women were adulteresses, liars, and even a prostitute, yet Matthew chose these women to be mentioned in Jesus' genealogy. Why? He wanted to show that Jesus came to redeem the past of women no matter how bad it might have been. In biblical times, like in many situations today, society had a double standard. A man could have an indiscretion and go right on with his future. A woman was forever marked. God let the story of the woman at the well be recorded and even mentioned these women with a past in the Bible because He is a God of second chances. The devil will try to get us to live in the shame of our past, canceling any hopes of a profitable present or future. God, on the other hand, will even use your past testimony to lead others to Christ or to set them free from bondage. He forgives, erases our pasts, and gives us back our self-respect and dignity so we can go out and help other people. No matter what your past, you can be used by Christ because Jesus takes all shame and guilt from you. Put more precisely, Jesus changes the world of women so they can go on and change the world. There are people waiting for you; now you can bring to others what Jesus did to heal and set you free.

Some other special distinctions of women in the Bible:

They were last at the cross. The women were the last to leave the crucifixion scene. "And Mary Magdalene and Mary the mother of Jesus observed where He was laid." (Mark 15:47) What happened to all of the men? All of the male disciples, except for John, forsook their master and fled.

The women were first at the tomb. "NOW ON the first day of the week, Mary Magdalene came to the tomb early, while it was still dark, and saw that the stone had been removed from (lifted out of the groove across the entrance of) the tomb." (John 20:1, AMP) Peter and John came looking, but went home. Mary stayed on alone and later actually encountered the risen Lord in the garden.

It was a woman who was the first to proclaim the resurrection. "Now when He arose early on the first day of the week, He appeared first to Mary Magdalene, out of whom He had cast seven demons. She went and told those who had been with Him, as they mourned and wept." (Mark 16:9-10) He then commissioned her to testify to this truth.

When the Apollo spacecraft first landed on the moon, President Nixon announced that, "This was the greatest event since the creation of the world." Billy Graham received national attention when he openly contradicted the President by saying, "The greatest event in the history of the world was the resurrection of Jesus Christ!" I personally agree that the resurrection was indeed the greatest all-time event, and I stand amazed that God deliberately revealed this to a woman. Jesus viewed women as full persons with real value. Unlike most of the males of His day, Jesus was concerned (and still is) that women find fulfillment, surmount difficulties, and make the most of their lives. What did the coming of Jesus Christ do for women? The same thing it did for men. It released them from the bondage to sin and the fear of man. It also opened the door to freedom in personal relationships with God and one another. Each of us must remember that it is more important to be an individual of significance for God's Kingdom than to be a success by the world's standards; therefore, just as you were set free, you must carry that freedom on to others who are held in bondage.

George Watkins, in his book, <u>Women in Today's Church</u>, concludes all this bias that has held women back by saying,

> In this day in which we face the greatest challenge in the history of mankind, it is foolish for the church of Jesus Christ to disqualify at least half of its army because they are not the right sex. If the Lord God of Hosts has called them into His service, who are we to dare refuse to train them or allow them to do battle for Him? A man who is confident of who he is in God is not

afraid to allow a woman to take her rightful place of ministry. 'Together,' they are unbeatable!

Chapter Three

IS IT SCRIPTURAL FOR WOMEN
TO TEACH AND PREACH?

There is nothing worse for a woman who feels a fire burning or stirring in her heart to do something for the Lord than to be told, "Don't you know the Bible says, 'Women are to be silent in the church'?" Or, "According to Timothy, a woman can't teach." I can't tell you the countless times this has happened to me personally as well as to a host of other women ministers I have talked with. I never wanted to be a minister. I was very comfortable and confident sitting in the pew, praying for my husband when he preached. But as I said before, God matched me with the perfect man who saw in me the gift of teaching, the desire to be a missionary, etc. He was relentless until I finally gave in and accepted it. It was through his prayers and correct teaching of the scriptures that I learned that I, as a woman, could do anything of significance for the Lord as long as He assigned me the call.

I had been incorrectly taught scriptures that were keeping me from ever ministering. In fact, when I first got saved, I was told that women didn't minister -- except to women and children. I even wrote in my Bible, "Peggy, you must not teach, only share as the Lord leads, and keep it to the children and other women. Your ministry is to your family." I have since scribbled that out!!

For years, men and women have incorrectly read I Corinthians 14:34-35 which begins by saying that women are to be silent in church, and I Timothy

2:11-12 that states that a woman should not teach, and I Corinthians 11:3 which says that the head of the woman is the man. These verses are used to incorrectly justify why women can't minister. Many women read these scriptures literally and out of context and think that they are going against the Word if they teach or minister.

If you do not study these three scriptures in detail and in the proper context, you would think that Paul had no use for women. But I am going to provide you with many informative scriptures and facts that show this not to be true. As I dug into the Word, I learned that Paul actually commended a lot of women -- some of whom I never even knew were women because of their unusual names. He noted them for their work with him in spreading the gospel -- women such as Euodias, Syntyche, Junia, and many others.

Well, you might ask, how can one scripture say no to women preaching and then you find another talking about a woman preaching? Is God a God of confusion? The answer is simple. There is a law of scriptural interpretation which states, "Every scripture must be interpreted in the light of what other scriptures say on the same subject. Each passage must harmonize with all other scriptures." Men can lift verses out of their settings or culture, ignoring this law, and make them say anything they want. But one scripture cannot contradict another. How can Paul be saying that women can't teach and have to be silent when even he himself lists women who fulfilled all the five-fold ministry gifts?

These scriptures have been used to keep women from their calling because they were misunderstood, and the result was, and is, a shortage of laborers in God's army. As we learned in the previous chapter, the Jewish attitude toward women led to some radically oppressive misapplication of the scriptures. Remember, it was the Talmud, the Jewish interpretation of the first five books of the Bible, that made women inferior to men and prohibited them from speaking in public or being taught. This is why there are so many men versus women in the Bible. It was not because God preferred men over women, it was because of what man's pride and prejudice dictated. Jesus demonstrated God's intent for women when He came and broke all their cultural traditions, customs and prejudices when He openly spoke and taught women and had it recorded for all to read. So what is the correct interpretation of these scriptures which are so often used to keep women silent and out of ministry? Let's begin with I Corinthians 14:34-35:

> Let your women keep silent in the churches: for it is not permitted unto them to speak; but they are commanded to be under obedience, as also saith the law. And if they will learn anything, let them ask their husbands at home; for it is a shame for women to speak in the church.

After extensive research, reading numerous articles, books, and Bible commentaries about these scriptures, I discovered that it is important to note that there is only one Greek word -- *aner* -- for man and husband and that there is only one Greek word -- *gyne* -- for woman and wife. So you must determine from the context whether a scripture is talking about women and men in general, or specifically about wives and husbands.

First Corinthians 14:35 could not be talking about women in general because it states, "If they will learn anything, let them ask their <u>husbands</u> at home." (emphasis added) Since all women don't have husbands, the passage should be translated, "let your wives keep silent in church."

If we look at this scripture in light of the whole letter of Paul to the Corinthians, we will understand why he said what he did. The church of Corinth was misusing the spiritual gifts. Because things were not being done properly, Paul had to step in and correct them. In I Corinthians 14:33, we read, "For God is not the author of confusion, but of peace, as in all the churches of the saints." He then goes on in verse thirty-four to tell the women to stop talking, which was adding to the problem of disorder. He doesn't say, "Women, stop preaching and teaching," he says they need to stop disrupting the services.

In the early churches, as well as in many foreign countries today, the custom was for men to sit on one side of the church and women to sit on the other. In some cases, as in the synagogues, women were even in a balcony while the men were below on the floor. Paul was dealing with the fact that the women were disrupting the service by calling out to their husbands to ask questions. That is why Paul said, "If you want to learn anything, be silent." When we remember that the women were not used to being taught, we understand why they did not know how to properly listen. Because the women had little or no education, Paul was giving them some very practical advice -- wait till you get home to ask your husbands about something you didn't understand.

If an interpretation of a scripture doesn't harmonize or agree with all other scriptures, then it is being interpreted incorrectly. This is why the book of Corinthians must be read in its entirety -- not just one chapter at a time.

Linda Wright, in her book, A Cord of Three Strands, states that this scripture could not be telling all women to be quiet or silent in the church because it would be a direct contradiction to Paul's previous advice to women in I Corinthians 11:5, "But every woman that prayeth or prophesieth with her head uncovered dishonoureth her head: for that is even all one as if she were shaven." Is it possible for a woman to pray and prophesy yet be silent at the same time? Strong's and Young's concordances, and Vine's Expository Dictionary of New Testament Words, give us explanations for the word "prophecy" which prove that it is not a silent activity: (1) speaking under divine inspiration, (2) publicly expounding, (3) revealing the mind and will of God, (4) flowing forth in a gift, (5) revealing the counsel and ways of God.

In summary, in this scripture, Paul was trying to establish order in the churches. One way he did that was to address the problem of the women talking during the service -- nothing more, nothing less. In fact, there are even etchings and paintings on the walls of some of the catacombs in Rome that depict women preaching and serving communion, disproving the idea that the early church practiced a "women should be seen but not heard" policy.

The correct interpretation of I Corinthians 14:34-35 should read:

> Let your women (wives) keep silent in the church for it is not permitted unto them to speak; but they are commanded to be under obedience as also saith the law (remember this is the Jewish interpretation of the Torah). And if they will learn anything, let them ask their husbands at home, for it is a shame for women (wives) to speak in the church.

The other scripture on this subject that is used to keep women from teaching is much like the first one. First Timothy 2:11-12 says, "Let the women learn in silence, with all subjection. But I suffer not a woman to teach, nor to usurp authority over the man, but to be in silence."

Once again it is important to note that biblical studies show that Paul is not talking to women in general, but to husbands and wives. He is saying wives are not to usurp their husbands' authority or teach them at home. A woman can be a strong leader outside the home, as long as she is under the authority of her husband when she is in the home. The scriptural order of authority in the home is: God over man and the man over the woman and children. If you break the pattern, very likely you will end up with a broken marriage. Where there are two in charge, there will be strife and confusion. It doesn't mean women aren't equal to their husbands; they certainly should have their own opinions and feelings and should be listened to and respected.

Marilyn Hickey, who co-pastors a church in Colorado with her husband, said that the Lord told her to love her husband and not to teach him in the home. However, when she is in the pulpit, she is neither male nor female -- but God's messenger with God's message. God showed this to her to help her understand why her husband never reacted positively at home when she shared with him what God had showed her even though he thought it was an outstanding revelation when he heard her share the same things at church.

"Authority" in this scripture is the Greek word *authentes*, meaning to act on one's own authority. So a woman can teach under her husband's (or pastor's or whoever is in charge) authority or covering if she is given permission. Again, we are discussing regulations concerning the women learning. When Paul says "let the women learn in silence," he is saying to ask their husbands at home so there will be peace in the service.

Scriptures must not contradict each other. Why would Paul tell all women that they could not teach when he commended Pheobe (Romans 16:1-2) as a deaconess and evangelist? How could Priscilla (Acts 18:26) serve as a pastor and a teacher of Apollos if she was to remain silent? How could Junia (Romans 16:7) have an apostolic ministry and not speak in the church? We will study these women in a future chapter to learn more about their ministries.

First Timothy 2:11-12 should therefore be interpreted: "Let the women (wives) learn in silence, but I suffer not a woman (wife) to teach, nor to usurp authority over the man (husband), but to be in silence." Thomas Oden, in his book, Essentials of Ministry, states:

> We do well to confess early that far too much of Christian tradition has been unrepresentatively male dominated in priesthood and has failed to recognize adequately God's call to women in ministry. Women have always been more ready to serve than the church has allowed. What they lacked was the opportunity. Theological arguments are high on the side of the ordination of women from, (1) scripture, (2) tradition, (3) reason, and (4) experience. It simply is unacceptable to assume that women, by virtue of their sex, are incapable of being empowered by God the Spirit to preach and provide pastoral care for the flock.

It was on the day of Pentecost when Jesus released the Holy Ghost to empower and carry on the work He had started. Acts 1:13-14 says:

> And when they were come in, they went up into the upper chamber, where they were abiding; both Peter and John and James and Andrew, Philip and Thomas, Bartholomew and Matthew, James the son of Alphaeus, and Simon the Zealot, and Judas the son of James. These all with one accord continued stedfastly in prayer, with the women,

and Mary the mother of Jesus, and with his brethren. (ASV, emphasis added)

It is important to note that Luke pointed out there were women included in this impartation of power. Acts 2:4 goes on to say, "And they were all filled with the Holy Spirit and began to speak with other tongues, as the Spirit gave them utterance." Obviously, the women received the same anointing as did the men since the passage specifically states that it fell upon all of them.

Charles Trombly, in his book <u>Who Says Women Can't Teach?</u>, says:

> It is tragic that I Timothy 2:12 is used against women called and appointed by God thus keeping them from their ministries. The primary purpose for the baptism of the Holy Spirit is "power" for the ministry. In Acts 2:4 the Holy Spirit descended on them "all" and they were "all" filled and "all" spoke in tongues. Did God baptize the women, including the mother of Jesus, in the Holy Spirit and then forbid them to exercise the power of the indwelling Spirit in ministry? Any idea that God could not or would not speak through a woman simply because she is "female" contradicts the whole New Testament teaching of Jesus Christ and the apostle Paul. Paul says in Galatians 3:28, "There is neither

Jew nor Greek; there is neither bond
nor free, there is neither male nor
female: for ye are all one in Christ
Jesus."

My former pastor, the late Lester Sumrall, was
frequently asked to comment about women being
pastors and holding other ministerial positions. He
would always quote Galatians 3:28. I remember
him saying, "Let's stop all this fighting about the
women and start working together to get this world
saved." His own wife, before he married her, was a
missionary and had a church. His sister and
mother, who together pastored a church in
Louisiana, led Jimmy Swaggart and his family to the
Lord. He knew what women could do when
appointed by God.

Kenneth Hagin said in his book, The Woman
Question, "I personally do not see any harm in a
woman filling any of the offices (five-fold ministry
gifts) in the church. I do believe it would be a little
more difficult for a woman to stand in the office of
pastor, yet I realize God would use them there."

George Watkins book, Women in Today's
Church, adds, "If the church of Jesus Christ would
ever grasp the full significance of the plan and
purpose of God for Christian women, it would
revolutionize the entire field of ministry."

First Timothy 2:13-15 continues:

For Adam was first formed, then
Eve. And Adam was not deceived,
but the woman being deceived was
in transgression. Not withstanding
she shall be saved in childbearing if
they continue in faith and charity

46

and holiness with sobriety.

This scripture was quoted to me when I was a young Christian as an explanation to why men were over the women and why the men were to do everything in ministry. The interpretation given to this scripture was that women were so easily deceived that they shouldn't be placed in positions of authority. I accepted it until I began to grow in the Lord and study the Word for myself. Adam was created first and was commanded to name the animals. To do this took time and Adam had to gain a knowledge of God's entire creation. He knew the snake and understood that it wasn't natural for the snake to come up and make deals over fruit. That is why he didn't come to Adam first or try to deceive him. Adam could not have been deceived. The Bible says the woman was deceived. She was not less intelligent than Adam; she was just newer. She didn't know all that he knew. She was no less valuable, but being newer, she was just more vulnerable. That is why Eve was more capable of being deceived.

In talking about this with my husband, he shared a revelation I had not thought about. In Genesis 2:16-17 where God told Adam not to eat of the fruit of a particular tree, Eve had not even been created. After Genesis 2:21-22 when she was created, the command was never again repeated. Apparently God left it as Adam's responsibility to tell Eve about the tree. This means that he heard directly from God, but she heard indirectly through a human source -- the difference between *logos* and *rhema*. Adam had received *rhema*, the direct word from God, while Eve had only received *logos*, the general

47

understanding she got secondhand. According to Romans 5:12, sin entered the world through one man's disobedience -- Adam's. Even though Eve was the first to eat the fruit, the consequences of sin are relegated to Adam because he willingly violated the *rhema* word from God, while Eve is only considered to have been deceived since her infraction was against her *logos* knowledge of God's requirements. So the beauty of the story is that the promise of redemption from sin for mankind was given to the woman, not the man. This leads us to I Timothy 2:15, "Notwithstanding she shall be saved in childbearing, if they continue in faith and charity and holiness with sobriety." God is saying, as we read in Genesis 3:15, "And I will put enmity between thee and the woman, and between thy seed and her seed; He shall bruise thy head and thou shalt bruise His heel." In other words, a promise was given to Eve from God, "There will come forth a seed from you (Eve) that will bring utter destruction to the serpent (Satan, as the curse and cause of the fall into sin), and salvation (redemption) to all mankind (which of course was Jesus Christ)." So Adam brought the curse by his disobedience, but Eve brought us out from under the curse. This is why Satan particularly hates women.

Paul's message in I Timothy 2:11-15 was written not to keep women in place, but to educate and elevate them to their rightful place. He was saying that women need to learn and be taught so they won't be deceived. Just as in I Corinthians 14:34-35, they must be silent and not interrupt to learn. So women, if you want to be in a teaching or leadership position, you must do as II Timothy 2:15

states, "Study to show yourself approved unto God, a workman that needeth not to be ashamed, rightly dividing the word of truth."

The last of the three scriptures that are often quoted to silence women and keep them from doing what God has called them to do is I Corinthians 11:3, "But I would have you know, that the head of every man is Christ and the head of the woman is the man; and the head of Christ is God." Once again, Bible scholars believe the word for "man" here should not be translated "man," but "husband." So it should read, "The head of the woman is the man (husband)" as Ephesians 5:23 states, "For the husband is the head of the wife." Many translations actually express this meaning directly.

In Ephesians 5:23 and again in I Corinthians 11:3, the Bible declares that the husband is the head of the wife, a phrase which is often misunderstood and wrongly interpreted and, therefore, erroneously applied. We often consider the term to mean that the husband is in some way superior to the wife. In actuality, the term has more to do with origin than with status. Perhaps it is easier to comprehend the concept if we think of the term "headwaters," meaning the source of a river. At the point where the river pours into the ocean, it may be a mighty waterway able to accommodate great ocean-going vessels; however, at its headwaters, it may be only a tiny tributary able to accommodate only tiny rowboats. Without the headwaters, the mighty river would never exist; however, it is the final product rather than the source itself which gives the river its significance. A man may be the head of one woman -- his own wife -- but not all women in general or even all the women in the church. This passage does not mean that women are subordinate to men. In the family, for the sake of order, wives are to acknowledge the husband as the one in final authority. A husband is to respect his wife and her opinions. There will be times that the husband will be wrong and that is why both opinions must be considered. After prayer if the husband still feels that his decision is the correct one, his is the final decision.

After we had our first two boys, I knew that the Lord was telling me that He had one more "little blessing" for us. When I told my husband, he said, "No, our quiver is full," referring to Psalm 127:4-5 which speaks of children as arrows in an archer's quiver. He wouldn't even consider the thought. Well, after crying, begging, and all other types of ridiculous behavior, I gave up and gave it to God. I told the Lord, "I quit. If You want another baby in this family, You are going to have to tell Delron, my husband, loud and clear!" Soon after, my husband went to Israel without me for a few weeks. When he walked in the door upon his arrival home, the first thing he said was, "God spoke to me. We are to have another child." Oh, how I rejoiced. Our last baby boy was born because my husband was open to hearing from the Lord and not because I forced him into my desire.

It is also important to remember that wives are to submit to their husbands, but a husband cannot contradict any of the Lord's commandments. There is a story of Smith Wigglesworth, a man used mightily of God, who is quoted as saying, "Under God, all I am in my entire ministry I owe to my dear wife." At one point in his life, however, he was very backslidden and told his wife that she couldn't go to church anymore. He said, "I know enough about the Bible to know that the man is the head of the wife. You are to obey me!" His wife smiled sweetly and said, "Now, Smith, you are the head of this house. Whatever you say goes. And you know I do that. But you are not my Lord. Jesus is my Lord, and the Bible tells us not to forsake the assembling of ourselves together. The Bible tells me to go to church, and I am going." She held her ground and instead of backsliding with her husband, she ended up seeing him come back to the Lord and have a powerful ministry because of her faithfulness to God.

Men who don't study I Corinthians 11:3 in context interpret it to say, "Men are the head of women in everything." But men are not above women in the Lord. Christ is her spiritual head. Therefore, she does not have a subordinate place in the Body of Christ. It is wrong to use this scripture to keep a woman from a position in the church or ministry. If God has called her, who is man to challenge and "recall" her?

Ann Graham Lotz, Billy Graham's daughter, recounted in an article how she had been treated harshly in one of her early speaking engagements where men were in the audience. She said several men in the room actually turned their chairs backwards from her to let her know their feelings about women preaching. She said that she returned home troubled, feeling compelled to seek God's face and guidance. She said, "I've never had a problem with women in ministry as I was, because

I knew God had commissioned me. But I was having a problem with their problem." She went on to say, "When I speak, if I speak with authority, it is the authority of the scriptures, it is the authority of the Holy Spirit." At the next meeting, she said to the audience of men and women:

I stand before you unashamed, simply a woman, not <u>with</u> authority, a woman <u>under</u> authority, a woman under the authority of my Lord, under the authority of my husband, under the authority of my pastor, and under the authority in this particular meeting of the men that invited me to speak." She told the audience, "What a wonderful thing to be commissioned by God to give out the news that Jesus Christ lives and that He is Lord! God forbid that anyone should ever tell a woman that she cannot preach, that she cannot teach, and she cannot give out God's Word if she has been commissioned. I would challenge you to acknowledge that women, as well as men, can be under compulsion, compelled by the love of God, locked in by the truth that we know, as we live in His world that we 'have' to give verbal expression, not just to our faith, but to our faith in the Word of God.

She concluded by saying, "I think Jeremiah can sum up how I feel as a woman in ministry: 'His word is in my heart like a burning fire, shut up in my bones. I am weary of holding it in, indeed I cannot, indeed I will not.'"

This sums up how I feel and how many women reading this book, I am sure, also feel. Your first responsibility is to your family -- certainly to your husband and certainly to your children. But if God has called you to minister and you are obedient and very careful to follow the leading of the Holy Spirit, He will dovetail your home life and your ministry together.

Chapter Four

WOMEN IN THE BIBLE WHO
LABORED FOR THE LORD

Of the almost eight billion people in the world, only thirty-two and a half percent consider themselves to be Christians. Eighty-nine percent have never personally accepted Jesus as their personal savior and fifteen percent have never even been told the gospel at all. Yet in the midst of a world desperate for the message of Christ -- where there are too few laborers to reach the more than four billion unreached people and where qualified personnel are sought but not found -- a controversy wages in the Christian community around the world as to whether one half of the adult Christians (women) can teach or preach. Many women in the past, as well as the present, have gone elsewhere to serve since they were not permitted to use their gifts in the church. Florence Nightingale (founder of the Red Cross) was quoted as saying, "I would have given the church my heart, my hand, my everything, but she would not have them. She told me to go back and do crochet in my mother's drawing room."

As I have said before, if I had not had my husband sent by God to teach and encourage me to fulfill the ministry God had for me, I would still be sitting in the pews. Oh, I might be teaching the children or doing a women's Bible study, but that is as far as it would go. I have talked to countless women who, like me, were seeking women mentors, but found none. As women, all we saw was that the majority of ministers were men and all the Bible exploits we heard preached about were done by men. We thanked God for the biblical heroes such as Paul, David ,and others, and for the great men of God of today; however, we were severely handicapped when it came to being presented with female role models. Consequently, women have not been encouraged because they do not see or haven't been taught about some of the heroines of the faith who did things for God that were also recorded.

Let's look at some women in the Bible who did some real work for the Lord. Paul talks about many of them as his co-laborers in the gospel. Considering their cultural limitations and the prejudice towards women, it is a miracle that there were any women ministers. In spite of these restrictions, God raised up these women, and they found their place in the Bible. My hope is to see God raising up women around the world who, like these women, will push through their cultural and gender restrictions and let God move through them.

In the Old Testament, we have several prophets who were women. One such prophetess was Huldah, whose story is found in II Chronicles chapter 34:20-28..

> And the king commanded Hilkiah, and Ahikam the son of Shaphan, and Abdon the son of Micah, and Shaphan the scribe, and Asaiah a servant of the king's, saying, Go, enquire of the LORD for me, and for them that are left in Israel and in Judah, concerning the words of the book that is found: for great is the

55

wrath of the LORD that is poured out upon us, because our fathers have not kept the word of the LORD, to do after all that is written in this book. And Hilkiah, and they that the king had appointed, went to Huldah the prophetess, the wife of Shallum the son of Tikvath, the son of Hasrah, keeper of the wardrobe; (now she dwelt in Jerusalem in the college:) and they spake to her to that effect. And she answered them, Thus saith the LORD God of Israel, Tell ye the man that sent you to me, Thus saith the LORD, Behold, I will bring evil upon this place, and upon the inhabitants thereof, even all the curses that are written in the book which they have read before the king of Judah: Because they have forsaken me, and have burned incense unto other gods, that they might provoke me to anger with all the works of their hands; therefore my wrath shall be poured out upon this place, and shall not be quenched. And as for the king of Judah, who sent you to enquire of the LORD, so shall ye say unto him, Thus saith the LORD God of Israel concerning the words which thou hast heard; Because thine heart was tender, and thou didst humble thyself before God, when thou heardest his words against this place, and against the inhabitants thereof, and humbledst thyself before me, and didst rend thy clothes, and weep before me; I have even heard thee also, saith the LORD. Behold, I will gather thee to thy fathers, and thou shalt be gathered to thy grave in peace, neither shall thine eyes see all the evil that I will bring upon this place, and upon the inhabitants of the same. So they brought the king word again.

God's primary means of communication in the Old Testament was through the prophets. This office was an honored one and required allegiance to God. Prophets and prophetesses as a group held high positions of leadership over God's people. Whereas priests pleaded with God on behalf of the people, prophets were used by God to guide the entire nation, particularly its leaders -- the priests and kings. Thus, prophetesses such as Miriam, Deborah, and others mentioned in the Bible brought leadership, exhortation, and correction to the highest levels of Israelite leadership: the kings, priests, and other prophets.

One seminary professor maintains that God uses a woman only when a man is not available, but Huldah's call was during the reign of King Josiah categorically disproving this wrong concept. When the Book of the Law was discovered, Josiah and his committee went directly to Huldah for advice rather than to either Zephaniah or Jeremiah -- both of whom were male prophets during this time. Huldah called Israel to obey the Torah and led the nation to its most significant reform in nearly a hundred years.

These men went to a woman for direction because she was called by God and they recognized and accepted her calling. Unlike people today, those living in the Old Testament times did not make a distinction between spiritual and secular leadership. In 2008, some of the same Christians who were delighted to see Sarah Palin run beside John McCain in the presidential election were also reluctant to welcome women to the pulpit on Sunday morning. When Gospel Today published an issue with women preachers on the cover more than one hundred Christian bookstores removed the magazine from their counters. How is it that we think that a woman could lead the most powerful country in the world but not a church? So the debate over whether God equips and calls women to serve in positions of spiritual leadership is not over!

Miriam was also a prophetess whom God raised up. She led the women in a celebration dance of praise and thanksgiving to the Lord after God had finally killed Pharaoh and the Egyptians by closing up the Red Sea, allowing the Israelites to escape. "And Miriam the prophetess, the sister of Aaron, took a timbrel in her hand; and all the women went out after her with timbrels and with dances." (Exodus 15:20) She had a prophetic ministry of praise and worship and was probably one of the most prominent women in the Hebrew scriptures. She was Moses' older sister and served with him in leadership over the multitude of Jewish people whom he had led out of slavery in Egypt. In Micah

58

6:4, the Lord included her among the leadership when He said, "For I brought thee up out of the land of Egypt, and redeemed thee out of the house of servants; and I set before thee Moses, Aaron and Miriam."

Deborah was another woman who played a significant roll in the Old Testament. Judges chapter four tells her story. She was a prophetess, meaning God spoke to her and she relayed His word to the people. She was also a judge, meaning she ruled on disputes that individuals brought to her to settle. Deborah was also called to be a warrior. In Judges 5:7, she is quoted as saying, "The inhabitants of the villages ceased, they ceased in Israel, until that I Deborah arose, that I arose a mother in Israel." The Lord told her to tell Barak to go fight against Sisera, but Barak told her he wouldn't go to war without her. He wanted her to be a "military leader" with him. Deborah said yes, because she knew this was God's will and she was not afraid. But she told Barak that when they won, he would relinquish the honor of capturing Sisera to a woman.

> And Barak said unto her, If thou wilt go with me, then I will go: but if thou wilt not go with me, then I will not go. And she said, I will surely go with thee: notwithstanding the journey that thou takest shall not be for thine honour; for the LORD shall sell Sisera into the hand of a woman. And Deborah arose, and went with Barak to Kedesh. (Judges 4: 8-9)

That is exactly what happened. Deborah is our example of a woman who came up with results instead of excuses -- something we women are great at giving the Lord, "I'm just a woman with no credentials or experience." But look at Deborah. The Bible says very little about her credentials other than the fact that she was a wife and mother (Judges 4:4, 5:7), neither of which qualified her to run a country. At a time when Israel was floundering and every man was doing what seemed right in his own eyes, God reached down and plucked out a woman of great faith who was willing to follow obediently after Him. Deborah is the only woman in the Bible who both ruled Israel and gave military orders to a man with God's blessing. Barak could have captured Sisera had he trusted God a little more. Deborah, on the other hand, because of her faith, was made a vessel of far greater use than anyone would have imagined. She was also a poetess. Some of you women may be used to write songs or poetry or to be musicians. A musician or author is just as important as a teacher or preacher. It may be your poem, song, or book that will forever touch a life. God says to us, "I didn't use you because you could, I used you because you would."

It is interesting that Deborah had a husband, yet he was not chosen to be the spiritual or national leader for Israel. Apparently, her husband didn't have a problem with Deborah's having a full-time position in the ministry. It is important that you are in one accord with your husband as far as what you want to do for the Lord. If he doesn't agree with what you are doing, pray for God to change his mind. I know many married women who are alone in what they are doing because their husbands don't have the call or burden that they do; however, through their prayers, their husbands either support or assist them. Many active Christian women have unsaved husbands, and in their cases, the men just let them do what they need to do.

Jael is a woman in the Bible that few know of, yet she was bravely used by God. After Deborah and Barak's army defeated Sisera's army, Sisera fled on foot. He ended up at the tent of Jael, the wife of Heber the Kenite. Judges 4:17-22 tells the account of how she killed him.

> But Sisera fled on foot to the tent of Jael, the wife of Heber the Kenite, for there was peace between Jabin the king of Hazor and the house of Heber the Kenite. And Jael went out to meet Sisera and said to him, Turn aside, my lord, turn aside to me; have no fear. So he turned aside to her into the tent, and she covered him with a rug. And he said to her, Give me, I pray you, a little water to drink for I am thirsty. And she opened a skin of milk and gave him a drink and covered him. And he said to her, Stand at the door of the tent, and if any man comes and asks you, Is there any man here? Tell him, No. But Jael, Heber's wife, took a tent pin and a hammer in her hand and went softly to him and drove the pin through his temple and into the ground; for he

was in a deep sleep from weariness. So he died. And behold, as Barak pursued Sisera, Jael came out to meet him and said to him, Come, and I will show you the man you seek. And when he came into her tent, behold, Sisera lay dead, and the tent pin was in his temples. (AMP)

Judges 5:24-26 adds, "Most blessed among women is Jael, the wife of Heber the Kenite; Blessed is she among women in tents. He asked for water; she gave milk; She brought out cream in a lordly bowl. She stretched her hand to the tent peg, Her right hand to the workmen's hammer; She pounded Sisera, she pierced his head, she split and struck through his temple." (NKJV) They called Jael "blessed above all women" for her heroic act, and in several verses it says that she had a husband. When you think of what she had to do -- killing the captain of the army -- you would normally think that God would use a man. But He called her to do it and even gave her a great plan of how to accomplish it. Most women would have never thought of using a hammer and a nail to kill someone -- much less have the courage to do it. But Jael had an assignment from God, and with His strength and boldness, accomplished what she was called to do. Because of her obedience, she went down in history. This truly is an encouragement to women that we can do whatever God calls us to do, no matter what it is.

I remember several years ago in Nepal, I was asked to preach at a church outside the city. When the car stopped, all I saw was a swinging bamboo bridge with no ropes to hang on to and a deep swift-moving river underneath. The pastor and congregation were waiting for me in the church on the other side. How was I going to get across that river on a bridge that had no handrail, not to mention that it was swinging back and forth as it hung over the cold and dangerous river? I told my interpreter that there must be another way to get to the church, but he answered, "No, this is it." Well, I froze. I thought, "I just can't do this, or if I do, I will end up in the river, floating downstream, able to only preach to the fish." As I began to tell the Lord that I just couldn't believe He would expect me to do this and surely He understood my fear and inability to do this preaching assignment, I heard one word, "Crawl!" I said back to the Lord, "Crawl across the bridge? Lord, I have on a dress and high-heels." Again I heard, "Crawl, and I will get you across to the other side." When I told my interpreter my plan, he just looked at me. I told him, "You are used to these bridges. If I walk across, I will fall in and there will be no preaching today. Take my shoes and Bible and let me do it my way." Well, I was the entertainment for the day as I started crawling, with the bridge swinging and my crying out to God. I finally made it to the other side with no incident, except for my total embarrassment at being the center of attention from the people who came from all over to see this silly white woman crawling across the bridge. Oh, did they ever have some good laughs! All that was soon to be forgotten as the Spirit of the living Lord moved in the service. The Word says in 1 Samuel 2:30, "But now the Lord says, Be it far from Me. For those who honor Me I will honor, and those who despise Me shall be lightly esteemed." (AMP) In the middle of my preaching, the pastor who was interpreting for me was slain in the Spirit and completely healed and set free of the effects of a traumatic event that had happened to him. He was "out" the entire service while the Holy Spirit worked on him. When he got up afterwards to share his testimony, I just cried to hear what God had done. What if I had let my fear of falling into the river take over and had turned around to go back to my hotel? Instead of that, I, like Jael, canceled my fear with faith and took God's hand and fulfilled my assignment.

Esther, another courageous lady called to do a great and heroic task for God, is discussed more later in this book. Once again, God affirmed the value of a woman by using an orphan girl with no special education or qualifications, to shine forth with faith, courage, and obedience to save her Jewish people from being destroyed. Her story, told in the book which bears her name, explains how she bravely accepted her uncle Mordecai's request to make a petition to the king to save her Hebrew people -- a move which could have resulted in her execution because she didn't have permission to appear before him without his first inviting her. What if she had said, "Oh, this is too hard, Lord. The king won't listen to me, and I could be killed if I don't have favor with him." But she knew that she was the one to complete the assignment and, as a woman, she was in the perfect position to influence the king and lead him to see the truth. So because of Esther's compliance, Haman's diabolical plans to completely destroy all Hebrews were stopped. Thus Esther went from being an orphan whom nobody knew, to a queen who became a heroine in history because she obeyed and trusted the Lord.

Many, many times God will call you to do things you can't do in your own natural abilities. However, the Lord will show you that although you are correct in saying that you can't do them, you can do anything through the ability of the One who called you to do it. Some of you have been given prophecies, dreams, and visions of the things that He has called you to do. When you look at yourself and your own abilities, you say, "How can it be?" You must keep saying, "I can't, but God can." When you face obstacles -- and you will -- keep saying as Paul did in Romans 8:31, "If God is for me, who can be against me?" Sometimes you may not understand why God has you in a particular job or situation that seems to have nothing to do with what you want to do spiritually for the Lord; however, later you will look back and see how that experience actually helped you with your present ministry. Also, God knows that you need to practice and prove yourself faithful before He puts you into your real calling. Many women in ministry started out as I did with seemingly unimportant roles -- yet He was watching, training, and preparing them for more!

The New Testament has another wonderful group of women whom God picked to serve Him amid the cultural impositions. For those of you who think that you are too old, Luke 2:36-38 tells us about an eighty-four year old widow named Anna.

And there was also a prophetess, Anna, the daughter of Phanuel, of the tribe of Asher. She was very old, having lived with her husband seven years from her maidenhood, And as a widow even for eighty-four years. She did not go out from the temple enclosure, but was worshiping night and day with fasting and prayer. And she too came up at that same hour, and she returned thanks to God and talked of [Jesus] to all who were looking for the redemption (deliverance) of Jerusalem. (AMP)

When Joseph and Mary brought the baby Jesus to the temple to be dedicated, Anna, because she was a prophetess, knew as soon as she saw Him that this was no ordinary baby. He was the Messiah they had all prayed and waited for. She began to praise and thank the Lord for allowing her to see the fruit of her and her people's prayers. When God's only Son came to be dedicated, Anna announced that their Savior and Redeemer had finally come. It is significant that God chose a woman, not a priest or a male teacher of the law, to express the joy and victory they all felt that day.

Philip, the evangelist, had four daughters who were prophetesses. Acts 21:8-9 says, "On the next day we who were Paul's companions departed and came to Caesarea, and entered the house of Philip the evangelist, who was one of the seven, and stayed with him. Now this man had four virgin daughters who prophesied." These four girls did more than just get up in the church and prophesy a little given the traditional definition of prophesy which is a message of encouragement, edification, or

66

comfort. That is the simple gift of prophecy. The Greek word used to describe the gifting that these girls had is *propheteuo* which, as mentioned before, means to foretell events, speak under inspiration, to exercise the prophetic office, and to be a prophet. The word literally means the official proclamation of the gospel of Jesus Christ, the prophetic voice of God. In other words, they were women of God. Eusebus, the historian, said that these young women traveled and evangelized throughout all the known world, preaching in parks and in public buildings and halls. They were a family team and powerful women of God.

Another prophetess was Elizabeth. When Mary visited Elizabeth during her pregnancy -- even though no one but Mary and Joseph knew that she had been chosen to give birth to the Messiah -- Elizabeth was used as a prophetess. Like Anna, the Lord revealed to her that Mary was carrying the Messiah. (Luke 1:39-45) Again, God chose a woman, Elizabeth, not her husband Zacharias who was a priest, to speak out this powerful word of knowledge and prophecy from the Lord.

In Acts 16:14-15, we read of Lydia who was an example of someone who did not have a full-time ministry and yet was used as the right person to open Europe to the gospel.

> One of those who listened to us was a woman named Lydia, from the city of Thyatira, a dealer in fabrics dyed in purple. She was [already] a worshiper of God, and the Lord opened her heart to pay attention to what was said by Paul. And when

she was baptized along with her household, she earnestly entreated us, saying, If in your opinion I am one really convinced [that Jesus is the Messiah and the Author of salvation] and that I will be faithful to the Lord, come to my house and stay. And she induced us [to do it]. (AMP)

Lydia was the first European Paul won to the Lord and she opened her home to him, and from there he won the continent. She used her position as a businesswoman to help establish the church in Philippi -- which was actually the first church on the continent of Europe -- and to support Paul as he spread the gospel. When Paul first came to the Roman colony of Philippi in Macedonia, he found a group of women who had gathered on the banks of the Gangites River to pray to the God of Israel because there was no synagogue in the city. Paul shared the gospel with them, and one of the women, Lydia, believed his message about Jesus. When Paul left the city, he left behind the early congregation with at least one very active woman -- Lydia.

Remember, ministry means any service to the Lord. It doesn't always mean that you have to be in the five-fold ministry as an apostle, prophet, teacher, evangelist, or pastor. Some of you will be in the business world where you will be able to witness, pray, or lay hands on people that would never come to church or have anything to do with a religious meeting. Some of you will use your finances as Lydia did to help churches, missionaries, and other

Christian workers or organizations to be able to do the work of the Lord. Both are pleasing to the Lord. Some of you may be in government or other positions of leadership where your influence or decisions will be the only light in the darkness. I have known many Christian women who were responsible for many great things being changed, or who brought forth great ideas from God. There is a saying, "Little hinges" open up big doors." For example, a group of Christian women, including myself, were fed up with the pornography in our town. There was a nationwide appeal made by a Christian radio program to march on a particular day with signs to stop pornography. We posted groups of women in strategic parts of the city to march with our signs saying, "Stop pornography." Yes, there were many who were not happy with our public display, but many cheered us on and the manager of the store we were near told us he would no longer sell this offensive material.

In the New Testament we find another interesting lady, Phoebe. Though she is mentioned only once in Romans 16:1-2, she seems to have played a very important role for Paul and the church.

> NOW I introduce and commend to you our sister Phoebe, a deaconess of the church at Cenchreae, That you may receive her in the Lord [with a Christian welcome], as saints (God's people) ought to receive one another. And help her in whatever matter she may require assistance from you, for she has been a helper of many including myself [shielding

us from suffering]. (AMP)

Eusebus, the historian who understood that particular era of early church history, states that Phoebe was widely traveled, that she had a legal mind, and that she would go to the courts of the land to argue cases for the churches. She was also an evangelist -- a public speaker. She was an overseer or superintendent of at least two churches -- one of them being a church at Cenchrea. As such, it was obvious that she was a woman in a position of authority. Paul also commended Phoebe to the church at Rome. This was an official endorsement of her ministry. Here was a powerful woman, recognized by one of the most prominent spiritual leaders in the church. Many scholars believe that since she is mentioned in Paul's commendations and salutations at the end of his letter to the Roman church which he wrote from Corinth that Phoebe probably carried this letter to Rome for Paul. If this is true, consider how important her fulfillment of this task was to the future of the church. He also asked them to receive her in the Lord and assist her in whatever business she had. Paul did not elaborate on what help she needed, but he did elaborate on the reason why the Roman church should help her. She was a true servant of the church. The word "servant" in Greek is *diakonos* from which we get the English word "deacon." She was a deaconess. Serving as a deacon or deaconess means to be a ruler or to be one having an area of authority. She is also noted as being a succourer of many and Paul said, "and of myself also." A ministry is recognized by its fruit. This word "succourer" means to bring help, relief, or assistance. She ministered to Paul, so he had been the object of her physical as well as spiritual aide.

Another passage in scripture which shows that women were involved in positions of leadership is Philippians 4:2-3.

I entreat and advise Euodia and I entreat and advise Syntyche to agree and to work in harmony in the Lord. And I exhort you too, [my] genuine yokefellow, help these [two women to keep on cooperating], for they have toiled along with me in [the spreading of] the good news (the Gospel), as have Clement and the rest of my fellow workers whose names are in the Book of Life. (AMP)

In this passage, we learn that Euodias and Syntyche were women who labored with Paul in the gospel. The Greek word for labor is *synathleo*, which means "to wrestle in company with, to seek jointly, to strive together." It implies the idea of struggling or fighting together as soldiers, struggling or fighting together side-by-side in a battle. They virtually shared his mission and struggle. There is no warrant to assume in the passage that there was any subordinate relationship; nothing except the full equality of men and women working together in the ministry of the gospel. He viewed them as fellow soldiers in the gospel, people whom he could trust because he saw the Holy Spirit ministering through them.

Priscilla and her husband Aquila are addressed

in Romans 16:3-5:

> Greet Priscilla and Aquila my
> helpers in Christ Jesus: Who have
> for my life laid down their own
> necks: unto whom not only I give
> thanks, but also all the churches of
> the Gentiles. Likewise greet the
> church that is in their house. Salute
> my wellbeloved Epaenetus, who is
> the firstfruits of Achaia unto Christ.

They had a team ministry of pastoring and teaching,
and -- as Paul mentioned -- even had a church in
their home. They were also co-workers with him.
This couple worked together with him, not only in the
ministry of the gospel, but in the tent-making and
leather-working business. They were partners in
ministry. Paul left them in Ephesus where they had
a great influence in the church by furthering and
instructing Apollos in the gospel. It is quite a
testimony to their effective ministry that they were
able to better instruct Apollos, who was already
mighty in the scriptures.

> And Paul after this tarried there yet
> a good while, and then took his
> leave of the brethren, and sailed
> thence into Syria, and with him
> Priscilla and Aquila; having shorn
> his head in Cenchrea: for he had a
> vow. And he came to Ephesus,
> and left them there: but he himself
> entered into the synagogue, and
> reasoned with the Jews...And a
> certain Jew named Apollos, born at
> Alexandria, an eloquent man, and

mighty in the scriptures, came to Ephesus. This man was instructed in the way of the Lord; and being fervent in the spirit, he spake and taught diligently the things of the Lord, knowing only the baptism of John. And he began to speak boldly in the synagogue: whom when Aquila and Priscilla had heard, they took him unto them, and expounded unto him the way of God more perfectly. (Acts 18:18-26)

Wherever Priscilla and Aquila went, whether to Corinth, Ephesus, or Rome, they were totally involved in the work of the church. Paul conveyed even more about the character of Priscilla and Aquila when he referred to them as his helpers in Christ Jesus, and then adding, "who have for my life laid down their own needs." Whatever the situation, Paul indicated that not only he, but all the churches should be grateful to them for their commitment to the Lord.

What can we learn about Priscilla from this overview? First, in every instance in the New Testament where Priscilla and Aquila are mentioned, they are mentioned together. They were partners in ministry. The fact that Priscilla is often mentioned first when the couple is named suggests that she was perhaps the more influential of the two as far as the ministry was concerned. Out of seven different translations, the King James is the only one that puts Aquila's name first. Dr. Yonggi Cho of South Korea comments that in the Orient of Paul's day, it was a disgrace to mention the woman's name first because the first-mentioned name indicated leadership or importance. He agreed therefore that since Priscilla's name preceded Aquila's in the majority of the different translations, we can safely conclude that Priscilla was more prominent than her husband. Many authors agree that through various historical writings and observations it seems clear that Priscilla was indeed a dominant minister and teacher. She and Aquila were co-workers, with the implication that the instruction was thus done by Priscilla. So here we not only find a woman in Acts 18:26 teaching a man (Apollos), which some would say is forbidden by I Timothy 2:12, but a woman teaching a man who was later to become a great leader in the church. Dr. Cho goes on to say that because Priscilla is mentioned first, that she was the leader in their house church -- she was the pastor, as it were, and Aquila was the assistant. She could pastor the home church because Paul had delegated his authority to her as well as to Aquila. I know of many churches where this is the case. The husbands are the administrators and feel very comfortable because they know that their wives were called by God to teach, so they come along side them. In the home, though, they are still the head, and their wives submit to them.

Junia was an apostle -- a woman who Paul said in Romans 16:7 was of note, "Salute Andronicus and Junia, my kinsmen, and my fellowprisoners, who are of note among the apostles, who also were in Christ before me." You need to realize that this does not say that the people just took note of these apostles, it actually means that they were noted apostles. What is the work of an apostle? To establish churches and to oversee these churches just as Paul did. There are over twenty-four apostles referred to in the New Testament, and all of them are people who were in positions of authority and leadership in the church. Junia was one of this group of chosen, anointed servants of the Lord. Historians say that Andronicus and Junia were probably a husband and wife team. Like Paul, she was a fellow prisoner. She had suffered incarceration for her faith in Christ. The church father Chrysostom writes, "and indeed to be apostles at all is a great thing. But to be even amongst these of note, just consider what a great compliment this is. They were of note owing to their works, to their achievements. Oh, how great is the devotion of this woman, that she should be even counted worthy of the name of apostle." That statement sums up Junia's story. But just think that most people don't even know that Junia was a woman's name.

Romans 16:6 says, "Greet Mary, who has worked so hard among you." (AMP) Mary here is mentioned among the laborers for God, and that does not mean she was in the kitchen or changing children's diapers. According to Dr. Cho, the women Paul was commending in chapter sixteen of Romans (Phoebe, Priscilla, and Junia, along with Mary) were laboring together in preaching the gospel.

Paul then mentions three more women in Romans 16:12, "Greet Tryphena and Tryphosa who worked for the Lord. Greet my dear friend Persis, another woman who has worked very hard in the Lord." (NIV) Again, these women were not just workers in the home as the Jewish men believed they should be. How do people labor in the Lord? They do it by witnessing, praying with people, preaching, and helping people spiritually.

We have mentioned and commented on women in every arena of ministry: prophetesses (Huldah, Miriam, Anna, Elizabeth, Philip's four daughters, and Deborah who was also a judge); evangelists (Phoebe, Euodias, Syntyche, Priscilla, Junia, Mary, Tryphena, and Tryphosa); a deaconess (Phebe); an apostle (Junia); a pastor (Priscilla); and teachers (Junia, Priscilla, and possibly several of the above women); though not specifically mentioned by name, some of these were sent out by Paul and were, therefore, also missionaries. This has been a long chapter, but one I took the time to write and research because I have seen that when I teach these truths women are amazed to find so many women in ministry who were busy working for the Lord during a time of history when women were so suppressed and hardly permitted to do anything. Paul has been falsely accused of saying that women have to be silent and cannot teach, when the book of Romans, chapter sixteen, and other books in the Bible have so much to say about so many women who labored for the Lord.

All these women and scriptures show that women have been called to gospel service and leadership from the beginning. Our God-given abilities and unique qualities will draw many to Christ because our power does not have human origins but comes from our Creator -- Christ.

Chapter Five

WOMEN OF THE TWENTIETH CENTURY

Aimee Semple McPherson (1890-1944)

Aimee Semple McPherson was one of the most remarkable, influential, and dynamic evangelists of the twentieth century. At a time in history when all the women preachers were sent to foreign countries since it was not believed that women could preach, she dared to step out regardless of the prevalent beliefs. She was an extraordinary, successful woman minister in a field dominated by men.

Born a Canadian in 1890, she was raised as a Methodist. At the age of seventeen, she attended a Pentecostal meeting held by an evangelist by the name of Robert Semple. It was there that she was born again and filled with the Holy Spirit. She then asked God what she could do and God gave her the scriptures Proverbs 11:30 and Daniel 12:3, "He that winneth souls is wise and shall shine as the stars forever." She wondered then how she, as a young Christian and a woman, could ever answer that call.

Then she started to question why women couldn't preach. She said, "Do skirts and trousers make so vast a difference? Women can instruct children, teach Sunday school, be missionaries, so why can't they preach?" When she went to the Bible, she read about Deborah, a judge, the woman at the well who preached the first salvation sermon and led an entire city to Christ, and the woman Mary Madgeline who delivered the first Easter message. Aimee went on to find that Apollos was taught by Priscilla. She also read of one man, Philip, who

77

had four daughters who prophesied. As she studied and prayed about how she, a farm girl, could ever become a soul-winner, she thought of Peter who was just a fisherman, but after he received the baptism of the Holy Spirit, had been transformed into an evangelist of power.

Aimee then fell in love with Robert Semple, the evangelist. Following a storybook romance, they were married. A few years later, they set sail for Hong Kong and China as missionaries. Three months after their arrival, Robert Semple became desperately ill and died. One month later, their daughter Roberta was born. With her six-week old daughter, Aimee returned to the United States.

After she arrived back in the States, she met and married Harold McPherson and became Aimee Semple McPherson. She described it as a marriage more of convenience and necessity than of love. She made the stipulation that if God should call her back into active ministry, she would go. Then she had a son, Rolf. All the while, a voice inside kept after her, "Preach the word. Do the work of an evangelist." "Impossible," she would say. "I have called thee and ordained thee a prophet unto the nations," echoed a voice. She became very ill due to her nerves from having the call of God on her life and not being able to do anything about it. One day when she was about to die, she heard a voice say, "Now will you go?" She then knew that she was headed either out to the mission field or to the grave. Instantly she was healed. She said it was interesting how all of the previous prayers from Christians did nothing while she was unwilling to heed the divine call. Then with a small cry, an obedient heart, and a change of mind, she was instantly made whole.

Those of you who have a call on your lives will never be satisfied until you fulfill it. You, like Aimee, may say, "I am just a simple woman, how can it come to pass?" All He wants is for you to say, "Yes," no matter what the cost. Let Him figure out and direct you to the next steps. I have met people who went after wealth, marriage, or careers instead of what God had spoken to them to do. To the world, they might look successful, but in God's eyes they failed to fulfill the destiny and plans He had for them. Therefore, they would never really feel satisfied. Material things only satisfy you temporarily, but being in the perfect will of your Father is where true contentment lies.

Aimee also showed us another area where we as women are particularly vulnerable. She married her first husband, Robert Semple, out of love and was equally yoked. He had a call to do the work of the Lord, and so did she. This was a true match made in heaven. The second marriage turned out to be quite the opposite. He was not in the ministry and she admitted that she married him out of convenience, wanting to be taken care of. All of this is understandable, but as Christian women we can't give in to those reasons. Aimee was miserable and ended up leaving him and taking her two children so she could go back to the call on her life. She asked him to join her, and two years later he came and saw what she was doing. By this time she had a tent and was holding revivals. After telling her to never stop what she was doing, he filed for a divorce.

Aimee's books are filled with wonderful stories of the things that the Lord did to and through her. One night, her tent was erected on a hill that a college used for a football field. Angry students formed a circle around the tent and began making loud, mocking noises. All Aimee and the team could do was sing. When Aimee asked the Lord what to do, He told her, "Begin praising Me out loud." She replied, "How can I when I feel like running away?" He said, "Do you praise Me because you feel like it or because I am worthy?" As she began to praise, she saw demons with bat-like wings back away from the tent; then angels came in and filled the canvas sanctuary. After she stopped singing and began to speak, there wasn't a sound. The tormentors stood quiet as mice. Many of them gave their hearts to Christ and brought their friends the following nights.

Even though Aimee was single more than she was married, she really was married to the Lord who always covered her, protected her, and provided for her every need. I often have women ask me, "How can I have a ministry when I am alone?" Others that are married and whose husbands are not called, or in some cases aren't even saved, ask how they can minister alone. I could give you lists of women, both from years ago and today, who pushed on through these types of situations and found the power of God to accomplish all things through and with Him. Being single or not having your husband in ministry with you doesn't have to be a problem if you know that you are really doing the work of the Lord with someone -- the Lord of Lords and King of Kings. You can't get a better partner than that!

Soon Aimee's ministry expanded to healing services. Many times, thousands of people would be jammed into the auditoriums while thousands more had to be turned away. She would hold two or three services a day for weeks. She stressed to the press that she was not a healer (as they called her), but an office girl introducing sufferers to the Great Physician. She then formed the Foursquare Gospel Church in California and built the famous Angelus Temple.

One night before she had arrived at a meeting, the newspaper headlined her arrival and said, "Miracle Woman Here." When she peeked out before she was to speak and saw all the stretchers and wheelchairs, she nearly fainted. She ran down and said, "Oh, Lord, I can't heal them." Then the Lord spoke to her heart, "If those sick people are healed and saved, who is going to save and heal them?" "You are, Lord, of course," she said. "I couldn't save or heal one of them." "Then why are you nervous? Just go up there and open the Bible! You know the scriptures on healing and salvation. You tell the people what I am going to do, and when you lay your hands on them, I will lay My hand on yours and all the time you are standing there, I will be standing right in back of you. And when you speak the Word, I will send the power of the Holy Ghost. You are simply the mouthpiece of the telephone. You are the key on the typewriter. You are only a mouth through which the Holy Ghost can speak. Will you go now?" She said, "Yes, Lord, and if they are not healed, it is Your business." There were more healings that day than she had witnessed in any other place.

Then the Lord told her, "If at any time people try to call you the 'Miracle Woman,' and to say you healed them, you will have no power. Whatever the results are, you are to say, 'The glory belongs to the Lord.'" What a powerful message and lesson we can all remember forever when we minister. God will not share His glory with anyone. If we can think of ourselves as merely conduits that the Lord flows through to others, He will allow much to be done through us. But we must always check ourselves for the pride that Satan will try to bring in. He knows that "pride goes before destruction, and a haughty spirit before a fall." (Proverbs 16:18, AMP) When you study some of the great men who had huge ministries, you will see how the pride and glory took them over and soon took them out.

In 1930, Aimee, at the age of forty, was at the height of her career, but she was lonely and let her heart mislead her again. Imagine coming to your room alone night after night after a huge meeting. She was vulnerable, and Satan deceived her once again into marrying the wrong man. His name was Dave Hutton, her third and last husband. She thought he would help her with her ministry, as he said he would. She thought it might be protection, a home, and love, but it didn't work out that way. He spent a short time ministering with her, then went back to the business world and, after a time, divorced her and married again. Jeremiah 17:9 says, "The heart is deceitful above all things, And desperately wicked; Who can know it?"

In 1922, Aimee was the first American woman to hold a radio broadcast license and the first woman to preach over the radio. She authored many inspirational books, songs, dramas, and operas. She was strongly involved in civic and community affairs, and traveled often as a missionary. The list of accomplishments goes on and on. She was responsible for establishing hundreds of Foursquare Gospel churches which are scattered across the States as well as around the world. In 1986, a new Foursquare Church was opening somewhere in the world every six hours!

Angeles Temple in the city of Los Angeles that Aimee built became America's first superchurch, known for powerful meetings. She also started Life Bible College adjacent to the Temple. During the first year in the Temple, more than ten thousand persons answered altar calls to be born-again. For the next twenty years, the sanctuary was usually filled to capacity with persons anxious to see and hear the legendary woman evangelist. As in the early years, thousands of people had to be turned away for lack of seats. In those years, Aimee ministered to more than twenty thousand people each Sunday. In the beginning, she personally conducted twenty-one services per week (three meetings a day every day of the week).

Her dramatic services captured the imagination and curiosity of the public. In one service, Aimee, dressed as a policeman, drove onto the stage on a motorcycle, blew a whistle, and shouted, "Stop! You are going to hell!" These extravaganzas made her a celebrity from coast to coast and gained her press attention equal to that of any Hollywood star.

All was not drama and glamour at the Temple, however. In 1927, Angeles Temple's commissary was opened to feed the hungry and clothe the poor.

When the Depression hit the nation in 1929, the Temple fed and clothed more than one and a half million people in the Los Angeles area.

In 1944, after one of her ministry meetings her son came to her room the next morning and found her dead at the age of only fifty-four years. Her death certificate indicated she had died from shock and respiratory failure after she had taken some sleeping pills prescribed by a doctor.

What she accomplished for the Lord, many could only dream of. She gave a list of all the wonderful things and places she had been, from submarines to airplanes (which were a phenomenon in her time), but she said, "None is as thrilling as what is known by a soul-winner when sinners burst into tears and come down to the altar."

Her autobiography, The Story of My Life, along with other books by and about her, tell of her various adventures with the Lord. There is also a slide show titled, "Milkpail to the Pulpit" that you can get through the Foursquare Gospel Church in Los Angeles. Let me conclude about Aimee Semple McPherson with a quote from one of her sermons:

> One of Jesus' last words to us was,
> 'Go ye into all the world and preach
> the gospel to every creature.' He is
> still speaking these words to us
> today with the same urging, the
> same pulsating and vital command
> as He did more than nineteen
> hundred years ago...You don't need
> to be an orator. What God wants is
> plain people with the good news in
> their hearts, who are willing to go

and tell others. The love of winning souls for Jesus Christ sets a fire burning in one's bones. Soul winning is the most important thing in the world. All I have is on the altar for the Lord and while I have my life and strength, I will put my whole being into the carrying out of this great commission.
What a challenge and legacy Aimee left us. She is gone now, but we are here. Let's do our part and do what each of us can to help fulfill the Great Commission.

Kathryn Kuhlman (1907-1976)

Kathryn Kuhlman was another famous woman evangelist known for her great healing meetings. Benny Hinn openly talks about her being his mentor and wrote a book about her. You will see that his meetings are structured very similar to the way Kathryn held hers. She preached at a time, like Aimee Semple McPherson, when very few women dared to preach because of the prejudice against women preachers. She said in one of her books,

A lot of people seem to think that being a woman in the ministry means I have two strikes against me. I've never felt that way. I just lift my chin a little higher and act like I don't hear the insults. I didn't ask for this ministry. God knows I would much rather be doing something else. But He put me in the ministry and those who don't like having a woman preach should complain to God -- not me. It's just like that.

This is good advice for women to remember when you don't feel accepted or feel negativity against you because you are a woman in ministry.

Kathryn was born in Missouri in 1907. At age fourteen, the Holy Spirit touched her at church and she became born-again. She changed from that point on. At age sixteen, she left her home to stay with her sister and husband who were in ministry. She traveled with them for five years, and then at age twenty-one, gave her first sermon and began her own ministry. She teamed up with Helen, a piano player, and began traveling with her. Later she was ordained as a minister. Kathryn openly said many times that she always had an inferiority complex. She hated her freckles and would talk about using freckle cream to try to hide them. She said she did everything to get rid of them. But she told the Lord, "If You can use 'nothing,' then I offer You that nothing." Between the 1940s and 1970s, Kathryn traveled extensively around the United States and in many other countries holding healing crusades. She preached at the Denver Revival Tabernacle for years. In 1937 Burroughs Wallrup, a married minister, came to preach at the Tabernacle. Through this encounter, the most promising young woman evangelist in the world would temporarily destroy her career. This is a story that we as women, whether single or married, can surely learn from. Her friends told her that it was wrong to be romantically involved with him, but she was determined to do things her own way, regardless of what God or His people thought about it. It has been said of her life, "If Kathryn had one great weakness in her long and fruitful career, it was her refusal to submit herself to the godly people around her. The whole idea threatened her."

I have stressed before that submission provides a covering and protection. It goes against our flesh not to do things our way, but God speaks, guides, and warns us when we are getting off track and being deceived. His warnings come not only through His own voice, but also through the voices of others who speak the wisdom He has given to them. Through submission, Kathryn would have found the needed checks and balances for the decisions in her personal life. But headstrong and independent, she plunged ahead and married Burroughs, who left his wife and children, insisting to her friends who were against the marriage that his wife had deserted him.

The two decided to combine their ministries. She was like Samson who had his hair cut. She was asked to leave the Denver Tabernacle, her long-time friend and piano player resigned and for the next eight years she "wandered in the wilderness." Her friends reported that all she did was sit on the platform and cry. Churches would cancel her when they found out about her marrying a divorced man who had left his wife and children for her. After they had lived together for six years, Kathryn made a decision,

> I had to make a choice; would I serve the man I love or the God I love? I knew I could not serve God and live with Mr. Wallrup. No one

will ever know the pain of dying like I
know it, for I loved him more than I
loved life itself. And for a time, I
loved him even more than God. I
finally told him I had to leave. God
had never released me from that
original call.

She concluded by saying, "No one will ever
know what this ministry has cost me. Only Jesus."
The author interviewing her said that the power of
God was so great in the room while she was telling
him in detail about all of this, that he had to leave the
office. Had he stayed, he would have had to
remove his shoes in that holy place!

It took two more years for her to try to rebuild her
ministry before the next chapter in her life could
start. God then told her to buy airtime on a radio
station. She didn't worry about the cost, saying that
if God had told her to do the broadcast and had
given her the time, she would let Him worry about
the cost. It was a procedure that she followed the
rest of her life, and later she went on to do a weekly
TV program called, I Believe in Miracles.

In the beginning of her ministry Kathryn had but
one message -- "Ye must be born again." Later
came her healing ministry for which she is so well
known. She began to study and ask the Lord about
the physical manifestation of healing. She had
learned that the only way to find truth was to come in
sincerity and let the Lord give her the revelation from
His Word. So once again, she returned to the Bible
for her answer.

What a great guideline for all of us to follow.
She realized that when Jesus died, it was not only

for our sins, but our diseases, too! She then saw it was the Holy Spirit who was carrying on the work of Jesus. She taught that when Jesus was filled with the Holy Spirit, things began to happen. He was suddenly empowered to heal the sick and even raise the dead. She taught that after He died, He gave His followers the greatest promise of all -- the Holy Spirit. He said that the same Holy Spirit who had lived in Him would return to live in all those who opened their lives to His power. The same things that He had done, His followers would do, too. In fact, even greater things would be done because the Holy Spirit would not be limited, but would be free to enter all those who would receive Him.

I pray that you will get this revelation. It's not us doing the teaching, praying, and laying on of hands, but the power of the Holy Spirit within us pouring out of us to others. You don't have to feel a thing; just do whatever He puts before you to do by faith. The devil loves to whisper into our ears that we don't have enough faith, anointing, etc. Ignore him and just be child-like. My son, at only age fifteen, had his first miracle happen on a missionary trip to Peru. A deaf man's ear was instantly healed when he, in his child-like faith, believed for a miracle. He just trusted and believed. God did the rest. Remember, it is between God and the person who needs to be touched -- you are just the go-between. So you are not responsible for the outcome.

When Kathryn began teaching this new revelation that she learned, a lady was healed at one of her meetings even while she was still speaking. Word spread quickly, and Kathryn's healing ministry quickly rocketed to another level. She made the newspapers, and as her meetings increased in size and popularity, pastors started to accuse her of stealing their sheep, to which she replied that she was just feeding a flock of starving lambs. Redbook, a popular magazine at the time, then did an article on her which set her on the road to national prominence.

When Kathryn Kuhlman saw miracles or heard herself call them out at her meetings, she said she was just as amazed as the people who were healed. She was quoted as saying it was Zechariah 4:6, "Not by might, not by power, but by My Spirit saith the Lord." This she said was "the only explanation I have as to why miracles happen in my meetings." She went on to say:

> I'm not afraid of man or Satan, but I do have one fear lest I grieve the Holy Spirit. I die a thousand deaths before I walk out on the stage. I know better than anyone else how dependent I am on the Holy Spirit. Without the power of the Holy Spirit, I am sunk!

Kathryn never had healing lines. People were healed while she was preaching or when she had a word of knowledge about a particular illness. Some were even healed before the meeting while waiting in line to get a seat, or just being in the meeting. When asked why some were not healed at her meetings, she only answered, "I do not know, but that is one of the first questions I am going to ask the Lord when I go to heaven. There are some things in life which will always be unanswerable." Sometimes the unsaved and those who came to meetings refusing to believe in God or miracles were the ones who received miraculous healings, while some saints left without being healed.

Kathryn had a unique dramatic style in her gestures and when she was on the platform, she spoke slowly and overly enunciated her words. She said she did this because that is how she learned to overcome her childhood stuttering. As she became more well known because of her television broadcasts, her meetings grew to the point that hundreds of people had to be turned away. She would always say, "I hope you haven't come to see Kathryn Kuhlman, for a great secret I have learned is that God will not share His glory with anyone." When people or critics asked her about being a woman in ministry because it was contrary to the times, she would simply reply, "A woman's place is where God puts her. For me, it is this ministry. This is my place because God put me here." When challenged about I Timothy 2:11-12, where Paul says, "Let the women learn in silence with all subjection, but I suffer not a woman to teach, nor to usurp authority over the man, but to be in silence," Kathryn replied:

Let me give you something very simply. I am quite certain that if it was contrary to the will of God to let women preach, Paul certainly would have reprimanded Philip, in whose home he visited. Philip, you remember, had four daughters who were preachers (Acts 21:9). Now that's a houseful of preachers, I'll tell you! Paul visited Philip and all four daughters were there. They would not have missed seeing Paul for anything in the world. But I cannot find a single scripture that says that Paul forbade these four daughters to preach. Peter quotes Joel in Acts 2:17 saying in the closing hours of this dispensation, 'Not only will your sons prophesy and preach, but your daughters shall also prophesy and preach.' Powerful words. So what do we do about Paul's command for women to keep silent in the church? Look at the situation.

She went on to explain that the women were yelling out in the services since they were separated from the men by either sitting in balconies or sitting on separate sides of the meeting place. They were disrupting the services so Paul said, "Let the women be quiet." Kathryn concluded:

That did not mean, that women were inferior. Some of the greatest leaders in Hebrew history were women. I admire Deborah, a judge of early Israel. I admire Queen Esther. I admire Sarah. I admire Mary, the mother of Jesus. All strong women. It was Christianity that freed the woman from her subservient role. I have never understood how any woman could reject Christ, for it was Christ who gave dignity to women. Christians may have problems with a woman in ministry -- but Christ never did. He elevated us. He set us free. I am glad I am a woman.

Time Magazine called her "one of the most remarkable Christian charismatics in the United States." By the time that she died at the age of sixty-eight years old, she had ministered to millions of sick people. The nurse with her when she died reported that she turned and looked as a glow enveloped the bed. An indescribable peace seemed to fill the room and she was gone.

Ladies, if you are open to the move of the Holy Spirit, you are destined to see miracles. Kathryn was a pioneer. Now it is up to us to see it come to pass. Kathryn is gone, but the Holy Spirit is still alive! Most likely, most of you will never have the large following Kathryn had, and yet some of you reading this book just may. The point to remember is that "God is no respecter of persons." (Acts 10:34)

What God needs is ordinary people who will be sensitive to the Holy Spirit's leading. You don't need big meetings to see healings or salvations. God's healing power has flowed through me to heal people in elevators, on the beach, in grocery stores, and other unexpected places. Whenever I am open and take the time to step out in faith, I have always been met with the power of God to heal. Just as Kathryn said, "I am more amazed than the person healed because I know better than anybody that I had nothing to do with it."

There are people waiting for you. And a Holy Spirit waiting to flow through you to do great and mighty works for Him. Always remember, "To God and God alone be the glory."

Mother Teresa (1910-1997)

Mother Teresa has been called, "A gift from God to the poorest of the poor," and was known as the "Saint of the Gutters." Pope John Paul II said that she was a "woman who marked the history of this century." This list of praises could go on and on, yet Mother Teresa, if she were alive, would ask you to stop and give you one of her many precious and wise quotations. "The work is not mine, but God's. I am only a small pencil in His hand. God writes His letter of love to the world through an action like ours."

She was born Agnes Bojavhiu in Skopje in what is now Macedonia. Growing up, she was fascinated by stories of the lives of missionaries and their services. At the age of twelve, she felt that she had a call to a religious life. Being raised as a Catholic, she left home at age eighteen to join the Sisters of Loretto as a missionary. She never again saw her mother or sister. Agnes took her first religious vows as a nun and chose the name Teresa after the Catholic patron saint of missionaries. She started out by teaching children at a school, but became increasingly disturbed by the poverty surrounding her in Calcutta, where she was assigned. While riding on a train to Darjeeling, she experienced what she called, "the call within the call." She remembered, "I was to leave the convent and help the poor while living with them. It was an order."

Beginning her missionary work to the poor in 1948, she wrote in her diary that her first years were very difficult. She had no income and had to resort to begging for food and supplies. She said that she experienced doubt, loneliness, and the temptation to return to the comfort of convent life.

I chose Mother Teresa as one of the women of the twentieth century to write about because she was so honest, humble, open, and solely dedicated to the work of the Lord. When there are obstacles and you feel discouraged with whatever God has called you to do, it is good to think about women such as Mother Teresa who faced greater obstacles than most of us will ever experience. Her faith and obedience to God kept her going.

As her work with the poor increased, she asked for permission from the Vatican to start the congregation of nuns that would become the Missionaries of Charity. Its mission was to care for, in her own words, "the hungry, the naked, the homeless, the crippled, the blind, the leper, all those people who feel unwanted, unloved, uncared for throughout society, the people that have become a burden to the society and are shunned by everyone." This order of nuns now consists of more than four thousand women of various nationalities who work on five continents. There are six hundred and ten missions in one hundred and twenty-three countries including hospices; homes for people with HIV/AIDS, leprosy, and tuberculosis; soup kitchens; children and family counseling programs; and orphanages and schools.

Mother Teresa said that the worst misery is not hunger, not leprosy, but the feeling of being unwanted, rejected, and abandoned by everyone. She said that it is in the affluent Western world that she has discovered the worst cases of loneliness. In her own words:

We are looking for the human beings whom Christ identified with when He said in Matthew 25:34-40, 'Then the King will say to those on His right hand, 'Come, you blessed of My Father, inherit the kingdom prepared for you from the foundation of the world; for I was hungry and you gave Me food; I was thirsty and you gave Me drink; I was a stranger and you took Me in; I was naked and you clothed Me; I was sick and you visited Me; I was in prison and you came to Me.' Then the righteous will answer Him, saying, 'Lord, when did we see You hungry and feed You, or thirsty and give You drink? When did we see You a stranger and take You in or naked and clothe You? Or when did we see You sick or in prison, and come to You?' And the King will answer and say to them, 'Assuredly, I say to you, inasmuch as you did it to one of the least of these My brethren, you did it to Me."

In 1952 she opened the first Home for the Dying in an abandoned Hindu temple. She and the nuns roamed Calcutta's slums, scooping up destitute people lying in the gutters. My husband and I have seen these nuns in action. I was overwhelmed with the poverty and condition of people on the streets of Calcutta on my first mission trip to India in 1983. The city is dedicated by the Hindus to Kali, "the

96

goddess of death." And this is exactly what they have received -- death, poverty, and misery. I made the mistake of giving one of the beggars something and soon we had an entire group of people following us, begging for alms and food. I thought I was going to die! When I cried out to the Lord, "Father, these are your children, what should we do?" He gave me Deuteronomy 28:15-68 and explained to me that they were under a curse because of all their false gods. The Hindus worship three hundred and thirty-three million pagan gods. They do not hearken to the voice of the Lord God nor His commandments, so they must reap the consequences. Deuteronomy 28:15-17 states that, "But if you will not obey the voice of the Lord your God, being watchful to do all His commandments and His statutes which I command you this day, then all these curses shall come upon you and overtake you: Cursed shall you be in the city and cursed shall you be in the field. Cursed shall be your basket and your kneading trough." (AMP) The rest of the chapter describes the problems of those who do not worship the one true God. He told me that although He loves them, He was still bound to His word.

This is why my husband and I go as missionaries and preach the "Good News" to countries like India. When the Hindus reject Hinduism and accept Jesus as their only Lord and Savior, they begin to experience the blessings found in the first fourteen verses of Deuteronomy chapter twenty-eight.

When we saw the Missionaries of Charities with their little cots picking up people with such emaciated bodies, we wondered if there was life left in them at all. The nuns brought these people to the Home for the Dying where they could die with love, care, and dignity. Some received medical attention. One of the most important things they saw and received was the love of Jesus demonstrated by these kind missionaries of charity. Mother Teresa said and always taught those under her that they should "see Jesus in every human being." She said:

> Kindness has converted more people than zeal, science, or eloquence. Holiness grows so fast where there is kindness. The world is lost from want of sweetness and kindness. Do not forget -- we need each other.

A personal Indian friend who lives in Calcutta and was a good friend of Mother Teresa's told me that the greatest thing she did was to tell them about Jesus. Many Hindus were brought to know the one true living God, Jesus Christ, before they died. Mother Teresa was a humanitarian, but it was because of Jesus who lived inside of her. The four-foot, eleven-inch tall nun radiated pure, selfless goodness as she let the Jesus in her glow forth. In a world too often darkened by genocide, war, and cruel indifference, she was a beacon of Jesus' light and hope. She once said, "We are called not to be successful but faithful." And to that call she was faithful! "A beautiful death," she said, "is for people who lived like animals to die like angels -- loved and wanted."

Now you know why, although India is predominately Hindu, Mother Teresa was regarded as a national treasure who transcended religious divisions. India's former prime minister said, "The world, and especially India, is poorer by her passing away. Hers was a life devoted to bringing love, peace, and joy to people whom the world generally shuns."

During our first trip to Calcutta, I asked the Lord to make a way for me to meet Mother Teresa, and He did just that! My husband and I finally made our way to the convent where she lived. Because of her busy traveling schedule, we could only pray that we had picked a day she was at home. As we entered the simple, clean, concrete building, we immediately sensed the presence of God. What a sweet spirit was in that place. We never expected that we would actually have the privilege of talking with this great woman. We thought that perhaps we would get a welcome from one of the sisters there and a tour of the facility.

A nun warmly welcomed us and replied that Mother was busy in a meeting, but if we could wait a minute, she would ask Mother if she could see us. In just a few minutes, the door opened and she entered the room. This saint of God had dropped all that she was doing to visit with strangers who had shown up at her door unannounced and without an appointment or invitation! Her welcome to us was as heartfelt as if we were her closest friends or outstanding celebrities or officials. But that was Mother Teresa. To her, every human being was of ultimate worth -- royalty or street beggar, it seemed to make no difference to her. She graciously shared with us about her work around the world and her original call into the ministry to the poor in

Calcutta.

She then invited us to the Home for the Dying. I was overwhelmed with emotions and told her, with tears, how I wished that I could visit this wonderful work she was doing but had to decline. I explained to her that I thought I was dying from all the pain and misery I was experiencing from what we had seen on the city streets. I went on to tell her that I had never seen anything like this. She just patted my hand and told me that this was a normal reaction for my first trip. She said many come from other countries to help, but many find it too hard to live and face what Calcutta has and they end up leaving. She said again, "That's okay, dear. I understand." The glow in her eyes was a window straight to the heart; it told us that she really did understand. She knew not only the hurt of those on the street, but also the hurt of those from the outside who were strangers to this level of anguish. On his following trip to Calcutta, my husband did have an opportunity to visit the Home for the Dying where volunteers from around the world were caring for the destitute of the city. Then he made his way to the door where he had been welcomed before. This time, a handwritten note was posted, "Mother is not able to receive guests. She is in prayer." Apparently, only God Himself was more important to Mother Teresa than the humans who made a constant trail to her door and into her life.

As we talked about all that she had accomplished around the world, we never felt the slightest bit of pride or feeling of accomplishment from her -- just the overwhelming, gnawing feeling about a job that still was not yet done. Through the outstanding quality of that one conversation, she turned the discussion away from herself and began to ask us about the mission work that had brought us to India and the neighboring country of Sri Lanka. After a few more minutes, she politely mentioned that her staff were waiting for her in a meeting. We asked if we could have a photograph taken with her before she left. When the picture was developed, we both laughed at the way we were stooped just like the aged saint. It was only later that we realized what had actually taken place. Mother Teresa was gentle and gracious, yet at the same time, she had such a powerful personality that we had actually begun to take on her qualities in just those few minutes. We could only pray that her faithful caring and loving would become evident in our lives as well. Her parting remarks to us were in reference to the necklace I was wearing. It was a metal piece which had a little dove symbolizing the Holy Spirit. "I see that you have the Holy Spirit. I do, too." Her life and works certainly proved it.

In 1979 she received the Nobel Peace Prize for her humanitarian work. She refused the conventional ceremonial banquet given to the laureates and asked that the $192,000 in funds be given to the poor in India, stating that earthly rewards were important only if they helped her reach the world's needy. Mother Teresa used her fame as a platform to speak out strongly for conservative values, arguing passionately against abortion, contraception, and divorce. In 1994 she spoke in Washington, DC, at the National Prayer Breakfast. She said how she felt that abortion was murder and went on to say, "If we accept that a mother can kill even her own child, how can we tell other people not to kill another?" She finished her speech with a standing ovation from the audience.

In regards to criticism, she was undeterred. When one man produced a documentary about her, entitled <u>Hell's Angel</u>, she told the newspaper that she forgave the producer. She said, "It is for you to decide how you want to live. As far as I am concerned, I know that I have to keep on doing my work." She said, "I work for the Lord and I have a clear conscience. No matter who says what, you should accept it with a smile and do your own work."

Another piece of advice she gave us on being a Christian was, "If you are humble, nothing will touch you; neither praise nor disgrace, because you know what you are." There has been so much I have learned from Mother Teresa. She has truly mentored me and impacted my life to serve the Lord at any cost. When asked where she found her strength and perseverance, she confessed, "I don't think there is anyone who needs God's help and grace as much as I do. Sometimes I feel so helpless and weak. I think that is why God uses me."

Many people didn't know, but she suffered with a severe heart condition. In 1983 she suffered her first heart attack and offered to resign at that time. She had offered to resign at other times also, but was always voted to stay. Her strength to go on came from the Lord. She was known as quite a prayer warrior. She often talked about the power of prayer and encouraged people to pray.

In 1997, just three months after she received the highest civilian honor bestowed by United States

Congress, she took her last breath and died. The nun with her said her last words were, "Jesus, I love you. Jesus, I love you." Truly, this was a woman who was not ashamed of the gospel of Jesus Christ. The Gallup polls during her lifetime and after her death, found her to be the single most widely admired person in the United States. In 1999, she was ranked as the most admired persons of the twentieth century by a poll in the United States. I believe this is because she was a mirror reflecting the love of Jesus. Love never fails. She truly reaped what she sowed to others. This was a woman loved by people all around the world for the love she so freely gave.

Mother Teresa's life story of achievements did not end until she was eighty-seven years of age. She was active to the very end, doing the Lord's work that others would never think of doing. She was given a state funeral by the Indian government in gratitude for her services to the poor in their country. Though she died the same week as Princess Diana, I told the press in a television interview, that I thought the real princess was Mother Teresa. Her example of self-sacrifice to others was priceless.

Summary and Conclusion

I could write an entire book on women of the twentieth century who have impacted my life as I have read about them and watched them in person, but Aimee Semple McPherson, Kathryn Kuhlman, and Mother Teresa are the three that stand out the most for me. These three were certainly three distinct and outstanding women, each with her own type of ministry. I was able to make a list of similar noteworthy qualities that I saw in all of them. None of us may ever attain the accomplishments for the Lord that these three attained, but an important question to you is, "Were you faithful to do what the Lord had on His mind for you to do?"

Remember the story of the talents in Matthew chapter twenty-five. To one servant was given five talents and to another only one. We could look at these women and feel discouraged, knowing that maybe even in five lifetimes we could never do what they did. That is a trick of the enemy to get you to do nothing because you feel it isn't important or valuable enough. We don't have to end up with a large ministry or go down in church history for what we have accomplished. Do what He has put on your heart. Most likely, what you feel drawn to do is from Him, and though you have fears about doing it, you will end up blessed and happy.

Be open to the Lord's desire for you. I never wanted to do missionary work or most of the things I am now doing in the ministry. When I met my future husband who was already doing short-term missionary trips, I had already decided I would be his helpmate by staying at home as his intercessor. I had such a fear of going. Vain imaginations totally had me bound. Getting up and speaking to a crowd was unthinkable to me. It was like Daniel having to go into the den of lions.

But God puts people in your lives who are going to challenge and stir up the gifts in you if you are open. I always told the Lord, "I will go where You want me to go and do what You want me to do. I am Yours. My life is no longer my own." Some of you reading this have probably told the Lord the same thing. Many times what happens next is that an opportunity to be used of the Lord will come along, or you will see a need, and instead of going out of your familiar, comfortable way of doing things, you let this God-given opportunity pass you by. Some of you are waiting for God, when really, He is waiting for you! I wanted to pray with people, tell of His goodness, and teach them what He taught me -- but when the subject of my going on a missionary trip with my husband came up, I froze. I always said, "I'm not ready yet." My husband wouldn't stop pressuring me to go, so I finally asked the Lord if I should go. He spoke to me and gave me Proverbs 29:25, "The fear of man brings a snare. But whoever trusts in the Lord shall be safe."

After I said yes, God was finally able to get things in line for me that He had planned. When I met T. L. Osborne, the great missionary statesman, I told him about my plans of going on my first missionary trip. With a smile on his face and a twinkle in his eye he said to me, "Honey, your life will never be the same." This was a prophetic word! I came back from my first missionary trip set free from the fear of man, and from that time until now, the doors to ministry have never stopped opening.

Aimee, Kathryn and Mother Teresa wrestled with the same thoughts as most of us. All three had to face their fears. We read about how each of them, before doing what God had called them to do, would realize that they were nothing without Him and the Holy Spirit's power. Aimee called herself just a farm girl; Kathryn talked about her inferiority complex; and Mother Teresa referred to herself as "nothing but a pencil in the hands of the Lord." Yet each one pushed through her personal weaknesses and found His strength and ability.

All three of these women showed great faith and obedience when God presented a task for them to do. Just obey that inner prompting. Don't worry about how it will all be done. Obedience combined with faith is the key. Just trust that God will do it!

There will be sacrifice involved. When you hear of accomplishments like these three had, it sounds so exciting. But remember that Aimee, Kathryn, and Mother Teresa all had to give up many things like a comfortable married life and had long hours of travel and ministry that they had to endure. They had to overcome loneliness, criticism, and many other mountains. Mother Teresa left everything and lived as a humble, poor person. She worked until the end with a severe heart condition that would have stopped most people, but she took the hand of the Lord and pressed on. Kathryn and Aimee, too, battled with health issues while in the ministry.

Aimee's and Kathryn's ministries both went to a new level after they received the baptism of the Holy Spirit. A good friend of Mother Teresa told us that she, too, was filled with the Holy Spirit. It is the Holy Spirit that gives us the power to do things for Christ that are impossible in the natural. They all three certainly could have written their own book of Acts of what the Holy Spirit did through them.

All three of these twentieth century women were quick to give God all the glory throughout their lives. It was their humility and practice of immediately giving the praise to God that kept these anointed women of integrity from falling.

Aimee and Kathryn both showed us, as women, how important it is to put a guard around your heart. The devil knows that single women are particularly susceptible to letting the wrong men into their lives -- men who could stop them or get them off track from what God has for them to do. At the Bible college where my husband and I taught, we saw many promising students with tremendous calls on their lives. The devil saw this, too, and tried to send in the wrong mate. Because she thought that life was passing her by, Kathryn talked herself into marrying a man who had shared her call to minister. Unfortunately, he already had a wife and children. Aimee let in two men who were able to temporarily hurt her ministry. She said that she was lonely and thought that a man could help her with her ministry. She had to leave both of them and admit that she had made a mistake. Had Aimee and Kathryn listened to godly counsel, a lot of pain and damage to their ministries could have been avoided.

Although these three women were praised and hailed during their lives and ministries, at the end they faced severe criticism. Remember Luke 6:26, "Woe unto you, when all men shall speak well of you! for so did their fathers to the false prophets." The devil is the accuser of the brethren, and he will always see to it that, no matter what you do for Christ, there will be critics to discourage you and even make you want to quit. Imagine all that Mother Teresa did and yet someone had the audacity to do a documentary, calling her "Hell's Angel." Aimee and Kathryn also had books written about them that made false accusations regarding their work. All three, I am sure, cried in private, but chose to let go and forgive in agreement with the Lord's command in Luke 6:27-28: "But I say to you who hear, Love your enemies, do good to those who hate you, bless those who curse you, and pray for those who spitefully use you." They let God handle their critics and refused to confront them, which would have drawn even more attention and criticism. We need to follow their example when we face these kinds of trials.

Let these and other women ministers, inspire, guide, and teach you. There is much more material on these women that you can get through the many books and videos that have been written or produced by or about them. When I went to the Billy Graham archives at Wheaton College in Illinois to study and watch videos of these women in active ministry, something just happened to me as a woman. My husband who truly appreciates and welcomes women in the ministry said that he enjoyed watching all the material we saw; however, it had a different impact on me. After we spent those hours in the archives, my life was forever touched and inspired. I just sat there with tears in my eyes, not wanting to leave. Only another woman would understand.

Women relate to women. We have the same emotions and heart. So after reviewing the videos in the archives, I left changed, inspired, and determined to do all I could for God -- no matter what obstacle I had to face or jump over. Since then I have taken hundreds of women to these same archives and watched them have the same reaction, "Look. A woman, an ordinary woman, and God did extraordinary things through her because God created women for the purpose of serving Him. If they can do it as a woman, so can I." Being a wife and mother are important ministries, but there is more waiting for you.

Chapter Six

ALL ABOUT THE ANOINTING

In the previous chapter, we studied Aimee Semple McPherson, Kathryn Kuhlman, and Mother Teresa; and saw that signs and wonders were evident in their ministries. None of these three women had special degrees that gave them the ability to accomplish the miraculous things they each did for the Kingdom. They simply knew about and tapped into the anointing of God through their relationship with the Holy Spirit. They knew and totally relied upon this anointing and were careful not to grieve the Holy Spirit by disobeying or being insensitive to His voice.

What is the anointing? What does it mean when people say, "Oh, she is so anointed?" How do you get it? Can you lose it? Can it be increased? We are going to study these questions and more in this chapter, because it is so important for you to understand the anointing and what it is and does. Whether you comprehend and want this one essential element for ministry will make all the difference in what you do for the Lord. This one component will separate you from an ordinary minister to one whose teaching will penetrate and change lives with fruit that will remain and whose ministry will be marked with signs and wonders as the Lord promised in Mark 16:17-18:

> And these signs shall follow them
> that believe; In my name shall they
> cast out devils; they shall speak with
> new tongues; They shall take up

serpents; and if they drink any deadly thing, it shall not hurt them; they shall lay hands on the sick, and they shall recover.

Often, the word "anointing" is used without the proper understanding of what it means. Many people who graduate from Bible college or seminary are almost universally convinced that their education has prepared them for ministry. They know little or nothing about the anointing of the Holy Spirit. The anointing does not come from a degree; it is not something you learn or earn; it is something that is given by God. Your success as a minister and your service to the Lord depends upon it!

Let's start by looking at how some people in the Old Testament received this anointing. In those days, actual oil was poured over the heads of those who were to be anointed for service to the Lord. This anointing with oil was a type or symbol of the Holy Spirit anointing that was to come later.

In Exodus 28, God told Moses to take Aaron and his sons and prepare them so that they might minister unto Him in the office of the priests. In verse forty-one of Exodus chapter twenty-eight, God told him to anoint, consecrate, and sanctify them. Verse seven of Exodus chapter twenty-nine says, "Then take the anointing oil and pour it on his head and anoint him." (AMP)

Another example of how the Lord anointed someone in His service is found in I Samuel 9:15-17 where the Lord told the prophet Samuel to anoint Saul to be king over the Israelites.

Now a day before Saul came, the Lord had revealed to Samuel in his ear, Tomorrow about this time I will send you a man from the land of Benjamin, and you shall anoint him to be leader over My people Israel; and he shall save them out of the hand of the Philistines. For I have looked upon the distress of My people, because their cry has come to Me. When Samuel saw Saul, the Lord told him, There is the man of whom I told you. He shall have authority over My people. (AMP)

First Samuel 10:1 says, "THEN SAMUEL took the vial of oil and poured it on Saul's head and kissed him and said, Has not the Lord anointed you to be prince over His heritage Israel?" (AMP) Verses six through nine explain what would happen as a result:

Then the Spirit of the Lord will come upon you mightily, and you will show yourself to be a prophet with them; and you will be turned into another man. When these signs meet you, do whatever you find to be done, for God is with you. You shall go down before me to Gilgal; and behold, I will come down to you to offer burnt offerings and to sacrifice peace offerings. You shall wait seven days until I come to you and show you what you shall do. And when [Saul] had turned his back to leave Samuel, God gave him another heart, and all these signs came to pass that day. (AMP)

For a while, Saul was a faithful, obedient king, but later because he did not obey God's commands, God removed the anointing He had given to King Saul and gave that anointing to David who succeeded Saul as the next king. This example proves that the anointing can be taken away. We will study more about this later.

In I Samuel 16:1, God instructed Samuel to fill his horn with oil and go find David. Verse thirteen says, "Then Samuel took the horn of oil and anointed David in the midst of his brothers; and the Spirit of the Lord came mightily upon David from that day forward. And Samuel arose and went to Ramah." (AMP)

Aaron and his sons went from obscurity to priestly power. Saul went from insignificance to a powerful king. David went from being a shepherd boy to a mighty king. Their lives were radically changed because they received the anointing from God. Even today, we can go from ordinary women to miraculous ministers when we receive this anointing as well. But how do we receive this anointing as believers in the New Testament?

We all receive a measure of the anointing when we ask Jesus to become the Lord of our lives. The name Christ or Messiah literally means "Anointed One." The anointing, then, is the touch of God upon a person's life for service. Jesus said that it was upon Him. It was the enabling influence that allowed Him to perform miracles. Acts 10:38 states, "How God anointed Jesus of Nazareth with the Holy Spirit and with power, who went about doing good and healing all who were oppressed by the devil, for God was with Him." When did He receive this anointing? In Luke 3:16, Jesus was baptized and filled with the Holy Spirit; in Luke 4:1, He was led into the wilderness by the Spirit; and in Luke 4:14, He returned in the power of the Spirit. This is why Jesus said in Luke 4:18, "The Spirit of the Lord is upon me because He hath anointed me." Before this power of the Holy Spirit came upon Him, He did not perform any miracles. Verse thirty-two of this same chapter of Luke says, "And they were astonished at His doctrine for His word was with power."

The anointing is much more than just a touch of God upon someone. This anointing is also the moving and operation of the Holy Spirit upon a preacher of the gospel to help him or her preach or teach effectively with real results. The anointing enables us to do miracles and to function in other gifts of the Spirit. It is the power given by the Holy Ghost when you embrace Him. Acts 1:8 says, "But you shall receive power (ability, efficiency, and might) when the Holy Ghost is come upon you and you shall be My witnesses in Jerusalem and all Judea and Samaria and to the end of the earth." (AMP)

If we have Christ inside us, we are actually filled with His anointing. However, just as the baptism of the Holy Spirit enabled Jesus to start performing miracles, we should make sure that we have the baptism of the Holy Spirit to receive the anointing power like He received. I have worked with other ministers who are not Spirit-filled and I have worked with those who have the baptism in the Holy Spirit -- and there is a distinct difference in their ministries.

Those who operate in the power of the Holy Spirit and have the gifts of the Holy Spirit operating through them see salvations, healings, deliverances, and miracles on a regular basis. They are not better than these other ministers who are also ministering and helping people; but, simply put, they have the power that the others are lacking.

When you minister under the anointing, the Holy Spirit takes your words and sends them as arrows into the hearts of the listeners. When they respond to the conviction that the anointed ministry brings, they see great changes occur in their lives. The anointing always creates a reaction.

People often ask me about my role as a chaplain at the jail. "Peggy, aren't you afraid when you go into the jail?" In the natural, I could easily be intimidated because I minister to hardened felons, some of whom are murderers. But when I go into the wards with Him and His anointing and remember that apart from Him and His power I can do nothing, my fear goes away.

This anointing of the Holy Spirit on a speaker is what makes people drive for miles to hear certain preachers, while others cannot draw enough listeners to justify opening the doors. People sense when the anointing is there and when it is not. No religion, other than Christianity, has this unction or anointing. Tragically, many of the denominational churches in the world have rejected the baptism in the Holy Spirit. Consequently, they have cut off, or at least dramatically reduced, the anointing of the Holy Spirit in their lives and ministries. As a result, little is accomplished despite great expenditures of money, effort, and time -- and sometimes noise and confusion. This is a major reason for a lack of results in the mission field by denominational missionaries.

When my husband and I were in Sri Lanka, we ministered at a church where many Buddhists were being baptized into Christianity. The denominational pastor who was letting our Spirit-filled friend use his church was upset and told him that he could no longer use his church when he saw all these baptisms. Afterwards, this pastor told us that it was because our Spirit-filled pastor friend had gotten more converts in just a few months than he had gotten in an entire year.

When God truly calls a woman to preach the gospel or serve Him in any other way, an anointing comes with that call. First John 2:20 in the Amplified Version says, "But you have been anointed by [you hold a sacred appointment from, you have been given an unction from] the Holy One, and you all know [the Truth] or you know all things." Verse twenty-seven goes on to say, "But as for you, the anointing (the sacred appointment, the unction) which you received from Him abides [permanently] in you; [so] then you have no need that anyone should instruct you. But just as His anointing teaches you concerning everything and is true and is no falsehood, so you must abide in (live in, never depart from) Him [being rooted in Him, knit to Him], just as [His anointing] has taught you [to do]."

Many times when you are ministering, you will be faced with demonic forces or people who need deliverance from demons. You must have this powerful anointing of the Holy Ghost to drive them out. So another purpose of the anointing is to break

Satan's power and the yokes of bondages and problems he puts on us. Lucifer, as Satan was called before he fell, was the first individual to be anointed in the scriptures. In Ezekiel 28:14, he was called the anointed cherub. His anointing came from being in the presence of God. When he was an angel, he was near to the throne of God, but he fell and lost his anointing. This is why we have the power and anointing to defeat him and destroy all his works.

Isaiah 10:27 says, "And it shall come to pass in that day, that his burden shall be taken away from off thy shoulders, and his yoke from off thy neck, and the yoke shall be destroyed because of the anointing." Can you see why the devil fights so hard to keep controversy and confusion about receiving the baptism of the Holy Spirit? In fact, some denominations actually have listened to Satan's lie and say, "The supernatural gifts are of the devil and have no place in the church today."

This study leads us to another common question: Can you lose your anointing? Three individuals in the Bible clearly answer this question for us. Satan was the first to receive the anointing and the first to have it taken away from him. This shows us clearly that the anointing and pride do not work together. Satan wanted to be like God.

> Your heart was proud and lifted up because of your beauty; you corrupted your wisdom for the sake of your splendor. I cast you to the ground; I lay you before kings, that they might gaze at you...All who know you among the people are

117

astonished and appalled at you; you have come to a horrible end and shall never return to being. (Ezekiel 28:17, 19, AMP)

Because Satan lost his anointing, he has no power over us.

Another person who lost his anointing was Samson who was set apart for the Lord as a child. His anointing manifested in his supernatural strength through which he was able to slay armies and do great feats to deliver Israel out of the hands of the Philistines. Judges 14:6 tells us, "And the Spirit of the Lord came mightily upon him." As a result, he was able to kill a lion with his bare hands. His life, unfortunately, was filled with wrong choices. His story is an example of how the anointing and lust cannot work together. In Judges 16:17-19, we learn about Delilah who became an instrument in the hands of Samson's enemies to bring him down. She was able to convince Samson to tell her the secret behind his strength. Then while he slept she had his hair shaved off. Verse nineteen says, "...And his strength (anointing) went from him." In the end, this once invincible man died as a blinded slave in the hands of his tormentors, the Philistines. This was all the tragic result of the loss of his anointing.

Whereas Samson was anointed to be judge in the Old Testament, Saul was called and anointed to be a king over Israel.

Now a day before Saul came, the Lord had revealed to Samuel in his ear, Tomorrow about this time I will send you a man from the land of

Benjamin, and you shall anoint him
to be leader over My people Israel;
and he shall save them out of the
hand of the Philistines. For I have
looked upon the distress of My
people, because their cry has come
to Me. (I Samuel 9:15-16, AMP)

At first Saul obeyed the prophet Samuel when
he would convey orders from the Lord to him. But
then King Saul decided he wanted to do things his
way, showing us that the anointing and disobedience
or rebellion cannot work together. Samuel gave
King Saul specific instructions from the Lord. In I
Samuel 15:3, he was told to go on a mission to smite
the Amalekites, Israel's enemy. The prophet clearly
told the king the Lord's command was to utterly
destroy all the Amalekites and not to spare anything.
But Saul decided that he would take the king of the
Amalekites alive and also save the best of the
animals. When the Lord saw this, He said to
Samuel in verse eleven, "I regret making Saul king,
for he has turned back from following me and has
not performed my commandments. And Samuel
was grieved and angry (with Saul) and he cried to
the Lord all night." (AMP) The prophet went on to
say in verse twenty-three, "For rebellion is as the sin
of witchcraft and stubbornness is as iniquity and
idolatry. Because you have rejected the word of the
Lord, He also has rejected you from being king."
God removed Saul from being king and replaced him
with David. I Samuel 16:13 says, "Then Samuel
took the horn of oil and anointed David in the midst
of his brothers, and the Spirit of the Lord came
mightily upon David from that time forward." As for

Saul, verse fourteen tells us, "But the Spirit of the Lord departed from Saul and an evil spirit from the Lord tormented and troubled him." (AMP)

You need to keep the anointing precious to you. Saul forgot this and had it taken away it, but there were men such as Elisha who knew how important the anointing was and asked God to even increase it. This leads us to the next discussion about the anointing -- can it be increased? The answer is yes, but there are some guidelines. When you start out to do what God has asked you to do, you will not get the anointing in full measure. Be faithful with a little, and you will get more. God needs to see if He can trust you with it. Will you still give Him the glory and realize that you have nothing to do with what God did for someone? Pride can come in so easily when we see God using us in signs and wonders.

The anointing can be increased. Elisha knew this and boldly asked Elijah for more. In II Kings 2:9, he said, "I pray you let a double portion of Your Spirit be upon me." Elisha had been serving Elijah and knew that the senior prophet had more anointing than he did. Elisha had a hunger and desire for his anointing to be even more powerful than that of his mentor. He did not run around and say, "Anoint me, anoint me!" He began to serve Elijah day and night and never said that he was too important to do even the smallest task. He was a faithful servant, as we must be if we are going to see our anointing increase!. It will be hard on your flesh and you need to die to yourself. Elijah said to Elisha when he asked for his anointing in II Kings 2:10, "You have asked a hard thing." Elisha finally got it; however, as he saw Elijah being taken up to heaven in a whirlwind. Verse twelve records that as he left, Elisha tore off his clothes, and in verse thirteen, the mantle (cloak) of Elijah fell on Elisha. He went on with an even greater anointing than Elijah -- just as he had sought after. Just as he tore off his clothes, we too have to take off our old clothes, which are symbolic of the things from the past that are hindering or holding us back from becoming the women of God He wants us to be. Be willing to go through hard times and stay faithful. First Peter 5:6 states, "Therefore humble yourselves under the mighty hand of God that in due season He may exalt you."

Remember, you are anointed whether you feel it or not. You can't work it up or earn it. I know some people who think if you don't fast before you minister, the anointing will not come. While fasting does make you more sensitive to the Spirit, it is not a prerequisite for the anointing. The anointing is there; take it by faith. You will see it flow stronger according to the expectation of the people or person you are ministering to. They, and their expectancy or lack thereof, set the atmosphere for miracles.

Once in my early years of ministry, I came home from a ministry meeting and told my husband that I had lost the anointing. I told him that the people were not receptive and that my message had accomplished absolutely nothing. He just laughed and tried to convince me it was the people's fault -- not mine that kept the anointing from being present at the meeting. The following week I did another meeting and gave the same message. This time the people were excited and we had a line of testimonies. The difference? The people's expectancy and faith.

These are the last days. Joel 2:28-29 tells us that God will pour out His Spirit upon all flesh.

> And afterward I will pour out My Spirit upon all flesh; and your sons and your daughters shall prophesy, your old men shall dream dreams, your young men shall see visions. Even upon the menservants and upon the maidservants in those days will I pour out My Spirit. (AMP)

I believe that He specifically mentions daughters and maidservants to let us know that, yes, women are included too. I believe for those who are expecting, we are going to go from a sprinkling of the anointing to a mighty outpouring with signs and wonders like we have never seen before!

Chapter Seven

UNDERSTANDING THE GIFTS

Did you know that everyone of you is a gift to the Body of Christ? This gift can only be unwrapped and given to others when you seek to find out your special endowment and ask God to release it. And this gift can only be of benefit if you use it when the opportunity comes.

I love mentoring other women. It is so rewarding to see the results after I teach the Women for the Harvest class. I can often see gifts lying dormant in women even when the women themselves do not see them. First Timothy 4:14 states, "Do not neglect the gift which is in you, [that special inward endowment] which was directly imparted to you [by the Holy Spirit] by prophetic utterance when the elders laid their hands upon you [at your ordination]." (AMP) Many people take this to mean that unless they are officially ordained, God will not give them gifts. This is not true. The Bible is full of examples of people who operated in the gifts even though they were not officially ordained into the ministry. The women we read about in chapter four whom Paul mentioned as evangelists, teachers, pastors, etc., were never written about as having been set apart, yet the gifts flowed through them. I have found that so many Christians look to their pastors or elders as the only ones worthy or eligible to have the gifts. They think that because they are not as mature in the Lord that they do not know what to do. They are afraid to step out and pray for people for whatever is needed. This simply is not right. Why would God tell us in II Timothy 1:6-7, "That is why I would remind you to stir up (rekindle the embers of, fan the flame of, and keep burning) the [gracious] gift of God, [the inner fire] that is in you by means of the laying on of my hands [with those of the elders at your ordination]. For God did not give us a spirit of timidity (of cowardice, of craven and cringing and fawning fear), but [He has given us a spirit] of power and of love and of calm and well-balanced mind and discipline and self-control." (AMP)

Again, if we look at the great ministers in the Bible, we will see that they had to deal with feelings of inferiority, fear, and incapability. God spoke to Moses in the book of Exodus and told him to go tell Pharaoh to let the Israelites go. In Exodus 3:11, "And Moses said to God, 'Who am I, that I should go to Pharaoh and bring the children of Israel out of Egypt?'" But God answered him in verse twelve, "I will certainly be with you..." This is what God still says to us today, just as He did to Moses. No matter what He calls you to do or where He places an open door, you are not alone -- He is with you to enable you to do what is required. Moses continued to try to convince God that he was not the man for the job. God loves to work through people who know in their own ability, they can do nothing. It is then that God gets all the glory.

In Exodus 4:10 we are told, "And Moses said to the Lord, 'O Lord I am not eloquent or a man of words, neither before nor since You have spoken to Your servant, for I am slow of speech and have a heavy and awkward tongue.'" Most Bible scholars take this to mean Moses had a stuttering problem. But the Lord went on to say in verses eleven and twelve, "And the Lord said to him, who has made man's mouth? Or who makes the dumb, or the deaf or seeing, or the blind? Is it not I, the Lord? Now therefore go, and I will be your mouth and will teach you what you may say." When Moses continued complaining, God was displeased and said that He would have Moses speak through Aaron. As it turned out, Moses finally did get over his fear and was used mightily by God to take the Israelites out of Egypt to the Promised Land. What if Moses had refused? There are people waiting for you just as there were people waiting for Moses. We all have to fight the fear of man, or of being rejected or misunderstood, when we step out in faith to do something for the Lord. How easy it would be just to sit back and ignore an inner prompting when He is asking us to do something. Remember that I Corinthians 14:1 tells us to eagerly pursue and cultivate the spiritual endowments (gifts).

We were created not just to be born-again and have a relationship with Him, but to bear fruit. John 15:16 says, "Ye have not chosen me, but I have chosen you, and ordained you, that ye should go and bring forth fruit, and that your fruit should remain: that whatsoever ye shall ask of the Father in my name, he may give it you." This is not a suggestion, but a command. When we ask in the name of Jesus, our gifts accomplish what we need them to do.

It doesn't matter what your gifts are. As the Body of Christ, we must all work and function together for the Body to be whole and complete. We must operate in what God has predetermined for us. We should not think of one gift as being more important than another. Just because a woman stands up at the pulpit preaching with people applauding her does not make her any more valuable than the people who interceded for her and the meeting. Both were very necessary for the people to receive something from the Lord. There are many things you will be called to do behind the scenes that no one but the Lord will recognize or appreciate. The ones with the gift that were publicly noticed and appreciated have already received their reward. Yours is yet to come!

So why don't people do as we were told in I Peter 4:10? "As each of you has received a gift (a particular spiritual talent, a gracious divine endowment), employ it for one another as [befits] good trustees of God's many-sided grace [faithful stewards of the extremely diverse powers and gifts granted to Christians by unmerited favor]." (AMP)

I believe that many people fail to use their gifts because they do not understand what the gifts that God gave us are or know how to function in them. God knew that we would need something other than our own abilities, so we need to learn how to take full advantage of the provision He has made for us.

There are three different sets of spiritual gifts that are mentioned in the Bible. I Corinthians 12:1 tells us, "Now about the spiritual gifts (the special endowments of supernatural energy), brethren, I do not want you to be misinformed." (AMP) We will begin with the nine gifts of the Holy Spirit which you receive when you are filled with the Holy Spirit. The listing of these gifts is found in I Corinthians 12:8-10.

> For to one is given by the Spirit the
> word of wisdom; to another the word

of knowledge by the same Spirit; to another faith by the same Spirit; to another the gifts of healing by the same Spirit; to another the working of miracles; to another prophecy; to another discerning of spirits; to another diverse kinds of tongues; to another interpretation of tongues.

The word of wisdom enables a person to make supernaturally wise choices or give information in the present that will positively affect the future. It is the sudden and miraculous giving of wisdom to meet a particular situation, answer a particular question, or verbalize a particular piece of knowledge. An example from the Old Testament would be Joseph's interpretation of Pharaoh's dream. This was not natural wisdom or wisdom through study and preparation, but Joseph was given an immediate supernatural answer.

The word of knowledge is the supernatural revelation of past, present, or future facts and an understanding about a present situation which we could not know naturally. An example of how this gift operates is found in II Kings 6:8-23 where Elisha, by a miraculous revelation, was given the location of the Syrian army's camp, thereby saving Israel from battle.

The gift of faith is when a person is given a supernatural trust in God to move in a situation. You just know that you know that God is going to intervene in a situation and do what needs to be done. Others around may not see how this could happen or are not totally convinced. Elijah is a shining example of this gift in the Old Testament.

He suddenly appeared on the scene in I Kings 17:1 and announced to King Ahab, the most wicked king Israel ever had, "As the Lord God of Israel liveth, before whom I stand, there shall not be dew nor rain these years, but according to my word." And surely enough, there was no rain for the next three years.

The gifts of healing are given to all of us in the Great Commission, but God gives some a special anointing for healings on a regular basis. Some even have a gift to heal a particular disease. Since there are many diseases, many gifts of healing are needed.

The working of miracles is when God supernaturally works through you to do such mighty acts as deliverance or other manifestations that show God's power. Some miracles in the Old Testament include the dividing of the Red Sea for the escape of the Children of Israel (Exodus 14:21-31) and the miraculous multiplication of oil in the widow's cruse and meal in her barrel throughout the time of the famine (I Kings 17:8-16).

The gift of prophecy enables the believer to speak a word of edification, exhortation, or comfort from the Lord to a situation or person he or she knows nothing about in the natural. What a wonderful example of prophecy we find in Isaiah chapter fifty-three where the prophet promises that Jesus would bear our griefs and carry our sorrows!

The discerning of spirits allows a person to discern between the operation of the Holy Spirit and demonic spirits in a person or situation. The story of Elisha and his servant Gehazi in II Kings chapter five is a good example of how Elisha discerned the dishonest spirit, and then through the word of knowledge, knew exactly what his servant had done.

Diverse kinds of tongues are given to a person, allowing them to speak in languages they do not know. On the Day of Pentecost, the believers in the Upper Room supernaturally spoke at least sixteen languages.

The interpretation of tongues gives a person the ability to understand an unknown tongue and translate the message into the language being spoken.

The passage concerning these supernatural gifts concludes in verse eleven of I Corinthians chapter twelve by saying, "All these [gifts, achievements, abilities] are inspired and brought to pass by one and the same [Holy] Spirit, Who apportions to each person individually [exactly] as He chooses." (AMP) So God chooses the gifts He wants you to have.

We are able to use them as we need them, but only if we are open and realize that we are candidates to receive these gifts. Some of you will be given a particular gift (or gifts) that you will use on a regular basis. Many times, you will see that there will be two or more functioning together. One example is when a prophetic word is given, it could also include the gift of wisdom or word of knowledge. Or when the gifts of healing are operating, the gift of miracles could be present. In the operation of the gift of miracles where a deliverance occurs, the discerning of spirits could also be operating to enable you to see if there is a demon that needs to be cast out.

Remember that you, not just those in leadership in your church, are given these gifts. Most of you will need these gifts outside of the church: in meetings, the work place, or wherever the Lord knows you require them to help to minister to someone.

These nine gifts can be divided into three groups. The spoken gifts encompass the diversity of tongues, the interpretation of tongues, and prophecy. These minister to us spiritually. The power gifts are the working of miracles, the gift of faith, and the gifts of healing. These minister to us physically. The revelation gifts include the word of knowledge, the word of wisdom, and the discerning of spirits. These minister to us emotionally.

The next set of gifts we will study are called the five-fold ministry gifts. These are given to people who are called into the ministry on a full-time basis. Since the majority of Christians are not called to these gifts, we must remember that we can still minister to others even though we are not in full-time ministry. The word ministry means serving God by serving His people however He chooses you to do it. These five callings or gifts are named in Ephesians 4:11-12:

> And he gave some, apostles; and some, prophets; and some, evangelists; and some, pastors and teachers; For the perfecting of the saints, for the work of the ministry, for the edifying of the body of Christ.

An easy way to remember what the five-fold gifts are and how they operate in the Body of Christ is to count them off using the fingers on your left hand.

First, your thumb represents the apostle. It can touch all the other fingers, just as this ministry touches all the other ministries of the five-fold listing. This is because a true apostle is one who can go into virgin territory for the Lord and raise up a ministry. To do this, the apostle must function first as a prophet to see the vision, then as an evangelist to win souls. Then the apostle needs to be a pastor who nurtures the people and a teacher who gets the people established in the word and their faith.

The prophet is represented by your index or pointer finger because he points us to the future. This brings revelation, knowledge, and direction to the church.

The evangelist is represented by your middle finger because it reaches out farther than your other fingers. The evangelist is a soul winner whose words bring conviction to sinners and encouragement to believers.

The pastor is represented by your fourth or ring finger. He is married to the flock. He or she exercises authority over the church by feeding, loving, and -- when necessary -- correcting them.

The teacher is represented by the little or fifth finger on the hand. This "pinky" finger is the only one small enough to get inside your ear. It brings a sense of balance to the rest of the five-fold ministry. The teacher's responsibility is to clarify truths to the Body of Christ.

Apostles, prophets, evangelists, pastors, and teachers all have been given to the church to edify and equip the saints and to help them mature in their Christian walks. It takes all five of these ministries working together to bring the Body to the place God has called it.

The key to finding your gift is total surrender.

Really, your life is not your own -- give it to Him. I never dreamed that one day I would have the gift of teaching. For some of you, these gifts are going to be a part of your future, too.

Only certain people are called to the five-fold ministry, but every born-again believer is called to the third set of ministry gifts that we find in Romans 12:4-8.

> For as we have many members in one body, and all members have not the same office: So we, being many, are one body in Christ, and every one members one of another. Having then gifts differing according to the grace that is given to us, whether prophecy, let us prophesy according to the proportion of faith; Or ministry, let us wait on our ministering: or he that teacheth, on teaching; Or he that exhorteth, on exhortation: he that giveth, let him do it with simplicity; he that ruleth, with diligence; he that sheweth mercy, with cheerfulness.

Each of us has one main foundational or motivational gift -- as they are called. Although you may have traits of the others, there will be only one or two that you will closely identify with. Jesus had all seven of these gifts. Seven is the number of completion in the Bible. When you see these seven gifts operating in the Body, you see His complete image.

Prophecy motivated people are very perceptive. They are also called perceivers as they have great spiritual insight into what motivates others. They see the motivation behind other's actions and can identify them as being good or evil. These people are very frank and direct verbally. The motivational or prophecy gift should not be confused with the ministerial position of a prophet or the gift of prophecy in I Corinthians 12:1. John the Baptist is a biblical example of this foundational gift of prophecy. A prophecy-motivated person always calls others to true repentance. If this is your gift, be certain to speak the truth in love and be led of the Holy Spirit. Sometimes, God will show you things about a person or situation strictly for you to intercede for them and not to confront.

The next gift is that of ministry, or the gift of helps. These people meet the practical needs in the church as well as for others. A server who is called into one of the five-fold ministries will be more successful than other ministers with the other foundational gifts because she is very practical in her approach. Servers already know how to meet people's needs, so they have an advantage. You must have the attitude of a servant in the five-fold ministry to be successful. Servers are alert to detect and meet needs as quickly as possible. It is just in their nature to help. The problem that servers have is saying no to everything that needs to be done. It is important to ask the Lord if you should say yes or no when asked to meet a need. Just because there is something that needs to be done doesn't mean that you are the one to do it. A person who has this ministry of helps needs to be recognized and to feel appreciated. For those of you who have this gift, there will be many times that you won't receive the recognition or appreciation. Just remember that God sees everything that you do for Him and He will reward you. A good example of a server in the Bible is Martha.

A person who has the motivational gift of teaching receives great joy from studying and researching the Word. Many times a teacher enjoys studying more than actually presenting biblical truths; therefore, this is not the same five-fold gift of teaching. These people prefer to use biblical examples rather than personal. They are very quick to catch scriptures that are used out of context and are very apt to correct those who interpret scriptures incorrectly. Teachers like to present their material in a systematic sequence. They need to be careful to present their material in an interesting way and to use some practical application. Teachers must also be careful not to let the facts become more important than the people to whom they are being presented. If you are a teacher, be sure to teach with humility and compassion, not just your intellect. Paul's foundational gift was teaching and he was also called to the five-fold ministry of a teacher.

An exhorter is one who is motivated to exhort or encourage people. Remember, the foundational gifts are what motivate you and what you do naturally. Exhorters want to see believers mature and grow in their relationship with God. They edify and encourage people and like to give steps of activity to bring others out of their problems. They like information from the Bible that has practical application. Exhorters are sensitive to others reactions as an indication as to whether the people they are ministering to are benefiting from what they are saying. They need a visible response, so they do better with an enthusiastic and responsive audience. Exhorters need not be discouraged when they don't always get this response, because many people may have received something from them but not have always shown it or exhorted them about how they liked their ministry. Barnabas is our biblical example. He followed and encouraged Paul.

A person who has the gift of giving loves to give freely, not only of her money, but also of her time and herself to the Lord's work. Givers desire to give quietly to effective ministries and projects. When they do, they feel they are knit spiritually to those ministries. They like to give without others knowing and do not want credit or acclaim. They also don't like being pressured into giving by appeal letters because they are already motivated to give. They are delighted when their offering is an answer to another's prayer. A biblical character that demonstrated this, is Abraham who gave generously to others and God.

A person with the gift of organization is one who rules or administers and is able to see the overall picture of what needs to be done in a situation and clarify long-range goals. Administrators are able to direct and lead others. With this gift, they are excellent communicators. They gain tremendous satisfaction in achieving their goals and involving others. They have an ability to know what can and cannot be delegated. They are also aware of the available resources to complete a task and have no problem getting people and resources together to get the job done. Nehemiah is our biblical example. He, with the help of the Israelites under his leadership, completed the wall that surrounded and protected their temple.

The last foundational gift is mercy. This person is full of compassion for others. Those with the gift of mercy have an ability to feel the atmosphere of joy or distress in an individual or group. They are actually attracted to people in distress and understand them. This type of person is very trusting and is also very trustworthy. They avoid conflict and confrontations. In a situation, they are able to discern the true motives of people. It is never their desire to hurt anyone, so they are very sensitive to their words and actions so as not to do so. When they see someone hurting, they love to minister the Word to set them free. The Good Samaritan is our biblical example.

All seven gifts have the same importance to the Body. Your gift is what motivates your actions. Some of you may never have realized that your personality trait is an actual gift to the Body. I have a friend that is a server, operating in the ministry of helps. She never realized that it was a gift she had. She just did what came to her naturally and didn't understand why everybody else didn't work right along side her. Statistics show that twenty percent of the people do eighty percent of the work that needs to be done. In other words, there are very few servers, but they get a lot accomplished for the Kingdom.

Knowing your gifts will also help you understand others. Others who do not have your motivational gift are consequently not motivated the way you are to do certain things. This can cause us to be judgmental or critical of others who don't behave as we do. Knowing this helps you understand, on the other hand, why you are drawn to certain people -- most likely those who have similar gifts to you.

If you don't know what your gifts are, ask the Lord. Young believers will have to take some time to recognize and let their gifts come to light. When I was first born-again, I really had no desire for the gifts. I was so focused on myself that at one meeting I attended, I realized that I really had little compassion for anyone but myself. As God began to heal me, I started to get His heart for others. As I grew to know Him, I became more like Him and saw more of the gifts in my life.

Though not everyone will be given the five-fold ministry gifts, all who receive the baptism of the Holy Spirit need to remember the nine gifts that come with it. They are yours and they are free. Matthew 10:8 says, "...Freely you have received, now freely give." The same is true of the seven foundational gifts in Romans 12:4-8. You all have at least one or two.

You will feel happy and fulfilled pouring out the talents God has given you. Don't let fear stop you! What happened to the man in Matthew 25:24-30 who was given one talent but never used it? He said, "I was afraid, so I hid my talent." Did the Lord say, "That is alright, I understand"? No! The Lord called him a wicked, lazy, and idle servant and ordered that he be thrown into outer darkness.

The Lord tells us in I Peter 4:10, "As each of you has received a gift (a particular spiritual talent, a gracious divine endowment), employ it for one another as [befits] good trustees of God's many-sided grace [faithful stewards of the extremely diverse powers and gifts granted to Christians by unmerited favor]." (AMP) We were created to follow Jesus' example in the Bible. He was always helping, healing, and trying to serve others in some way. If you are not truly satisfied as a Christian, one of the reasons could be that you are not using your talents to help others.

Many women say to me, "I know the gifts I have, but my church doesn't believe in women ministers." There are people everywhere waiting for you outside the church. Recently a woman came with her husband to install new counters in our kitchen. Her back had been badly hurt in an accident. Because I was obedient and stepped out in faith, God anointed me with the gift of healing and she left with a brand new back. The healing happened right in my kitchen, nowhere near our church!

The secret to your gift is grace -- the supernatural ability to do something you could never do. Jesus -- not me -- healed the lady in my kitchen, but He used my hands, prayer, and faith. In the same way, He needs your hands, your heart, and your mouth so He can flow through you to touch others. We are all He has. He wants to answer people's prayers. How does He do it many times? Through ordinary people just like you and me who dare to believe!

It is important to find your gift. I love to hear people sing, and at one point convinced myself that God had given me the anointing to sing. My family quickly corrected me and told me where He had called me. If you are called for a particular gift, then you will be anointed and there will be confirmation. I was at a meeting where I was to speak, and right before I came up on the stage, they had a special song. A little old man began to sing. He didn't have a strong singing voice, but as he sang, the presence of God was on Him so strongly that it brought most of us to tears. This was his gift. This was his calling and we were all touched.

Ephesians 2:10 says, "For we are his workmanship, created in Christ Jesus unto good works, which God hath before ordained that we should walk in them." This little poem, entitled Your Gift, brings all of this to a conclusion:

The Lord has given you a talent,
Though in some areas you may lack,
There is a skill at which you excel
One thing for which you have a knack.
Your gift may not be evident yet
Your ability may seem unclear
But the Lord will make it plain
Soon your gift will appear.
Your talent might look unimportant
It may not bring fortune or acclaim.
God's favor will be your fame.
Stay on the path you've chosen.
From God's direction do not drift.
In life you do not walk unarmed.
For God has given you a gift.

Ladies, you can't earn your gift or pick it -- it's a gift. Just discover it and accept it. It is not your gift until you open it and receive it. If you don't use it, you will lose it. How rewarding to read in Hebrews 6:10, "For God is not unrighteous to forget or overlook your labor and the love which you have shown for His name's sake in ministering to the needs of the saints (His own consecrated people), as you still do." (AMP) Nothing you do, be it big or small, will ever go unnoticed by the Lord.

Chapter Eight

PARTING FROM THE PAST

It is one thing to be convinced and confident that God has released and given you permission as a woman to do whatever He puts before you. The next step is to be truly free to accept your calling. Unless I had allowed God to go through some of the past chapters of my life and heal my deepest emotions, I would have never become a woman for the harvest. I embraced Luke 4:18 and let Him: heal my broken heart from past disappointments; deliver me in areas of my life where I was held captive in bondage; restore my sight where I was blind and help me to see the truth; heal me where I was bruised and hurt. Don't you want that too? Some of you have already experienced inner healing for things said or done to you, but some of you have never allowed the Lord to go there. You think that if you just don't think or talk about it and repress it, that it is taken care of. I can guarantee you it is not. Someone or something will cause it to come up to the surface.

Just as with a tea bag, your full flavor will not come out until you are put in hot water. Do you ever wonder why you or someone you know is overly sensitive in an area or over-reacts in a negative way in a situation? Joyce Meyer expresses it so well when she says, "Bad roots cause bad fruits." If anger, fear, low esteem, rejection, etc. are some of your constant companions, then you have a need for the Master's gentle, but awesome, touch of healing. Your wounded emotions become a prison that locks self in and others out. Jesus loves you and is especially interested in those who are bruised, wounded, and hurting.

Often, facing the past and dealing with it properly is more frightening than staying in bondage or prison. Not one of us would say we want to stay in bondage, yet I have met people that have learned to adapt to it so well that, when they were offered freedom, they are not sure it is worth accepting the offer. You do not have to be afraid to face some of the hurts in your life. Hebrews 4:15 says, "For we do not have a High Priest Who is unable to understand and sympathize and have a shared feeling with our weaknesses and infirmities and liability to the assaults of temptation, but One Who has been tempted in every respect as we are, yet without sinning." (AMP)

When my husband kept telling me that one day I was going to preach and minister, I kept telling him no because I did not want to deal with the root cause that kept me from taking my place in the ministry. I had a choice to make: was I going to admit that I had some fears and other issues to deal with and allow Jesus to walk me through the pain so I could come out into freedom, or was I going to let my pride, stubbornness, and rebellion stand in the way and refuse to deal with it and stay in my prison cell even though in reality, the door was already open? I had to choose to walk out and learn to deal with life according to what God's Word said about me. Getting well hurts because old wounds have to be opened up, cleaned out, and drained of all the poison.

I had a real fear of speaking in public.

According to authoritative studies, speaking in public is one of the major fears people experience. First, I had to admit my fear; then, I had to ask God why I was like this when it never bothered others. He took me back to an event in my early school years. I had spent weeks memorizing a poem that I was to recite at a big Parent/Teacher meeting at my school. I knew that poem forwards and backwards, so I didn't bother to write it on paper to bring up to the stage with me. Since I had not been on a stage before, I was not emotionally prepared to find everyone staring at and totally focused on me. When I was called up to speak, I completely "lost it," forgot everything I had so carefully memorized, began to cry, and ran off the stage. Totally humiliated, I said, "I will never speak to a group of people like that again -- never!" This experience locked me up so badly that whenever anyone even mentioned about me saying something in front of someone or a group, I got a terrible, panicky feeling and refused to do it. I just could not go through that pain and embarrassment again. Finally, one day my husband confronted me. "When are you going to let God set you free from that spirit of fear?" At first I got mad and denied it, telling him that he didn't know what he was talking about. But when I reluctantly asked the Lord if he was right, I got an answer I did not want to hear. "Yes," the Lord told me, "it is a spirit (stronghold) of fear that you let in as a child and have entertained for years."

I just didn't see how God could change my thinking, but I wanted to do something for God; therefore, I knew that this spirit of fear had to go. How could I tell others that Jesus was what they were looking for? How could I tell them that only He could satisfy their lives, fill their emptiness, and give them a reason to live when I was bound up with fear?

God showed me in Proverbs 29:25 that, "The fear of man brings a snare, but whoever leans on, trusts in, and puts his confidence in the Lord is safe and set on high." (AMP) I had some trusted elders pray for me and bind and cast out that spirit of fear. Then I had to begin to renew my mind with the Word of God. Romans 12:2 tells us, "Do not be conformed to this world (this age), [fashioned after and adapted to its external, superficial customs], but be transformed (changed) by the [entire] renewal of your mind [by its new ideals and its new attitude], so that you may prove [for yourselves] what is the good and acceptable and perfect will of God, even the thing which is good and acceptable and perfect [in His sight for you]." (AMP) I memorized scriptures on fear and who I was in Christ and began to meditate on them.

Then it was time! My husband told me that I was going on my first mission trip with him and to prepare a sermon. Oh, how I wanted to run back into my old prison of fear, shut the door, and throw away the key! Certainly God didn't need me -- wasn't my husband enough? But God was determined to finish what He started in me.

When we arrived in Sri Lanka, at first only my husband was asked to preach. Then one day the pastor at the largest church in Sri Lanka announced at lunch that the Lord had spoken to him that I, not my husband, was to speak at the evening service. There was my open door!

Ladies, inner healing and getting free are not fun, but if you don't fully cooperate with God, you won't get it. I had to walk through the door and say yes. Although it was as scary to me as going into Daniel's den of lions, I did it! I told the Lord that actually going into the den of lions would have been easier, but He assured me, like He was with Daniel, that He would be with me. When I spoke at the church that night, I saw that He keeps His promises.

I began to speak, and He kept filling my mouth with His words until it was time to close. I'm sure it was not one of the best sermons the Sri Lankans have ever heard, but I (well, the Lord and I) did it and that fear was put under my feet! That was the beginning of my ministry. When I returned home, I received a call asking me to speak at a Woman's Aglow meeting, and since then the invitations have not stopped. Why me? I wasn't some seasoned speaker. It was because of my trust, faith, and obedience. God will give you what you need to be successful. He doesn't produce failures. That was more than thirty years ago and He is still flowing through me. Does fear still try to come knocking at my door? Of course it does. The devil and my flesh want to quickly forget the new creature I am in Christ and dwell on the old me. But I don't let my mind go there. I speak the Word over myself and do what I have to do, knowing that it's Him (the Anointed One, my Messiah) that speaks and does all the work. I am just His yielded vessel through which He pours His love to others. This is why I want to declare "War" (**W**omen **A**nd **R**estoration) against our enemy, Satan, who has kept women from doing the Lord's work by making them feel that they could not possibly do anything of merit for the Lord.

I could write pages on how God has healed and restored me so that I could go on to become who He created me to be and fulfill my destiny. The important fact is that you have the same wonderful Father who wants to restore (to give back something taken or lost, to return to a former state) you as well as me. Second Corinthians 5:17 states, "Therefore if any person is [ingrafted] in Christ (the Messiah) he is a new creation (a new creature altogether); the old [previous moral and spiritual condition] has passed away. Behold, the fresh and new has come!" (AMP) Yes, all of us, when we are born again, become those new creatures in Christ, but many times we don't let those old things pass away. We have been given a new life and have been taken out of darkness and bondage; however, like Lazarus when he came back to life, we need to drop off those old grave clothes (old thought patterns) and put on all the confidence, courage, strength, and supernatural ability that God has for each of us. Joel 2:25 says, "And I will restore to you all the years that the locust (Satan) has eaten or taken from you." You must first be restored or you will never be able to use and release the anointing within you. Joel 2:28-29 says, "And afterwards I will pour out My Spirit upon all flesh; and your sons and daughters shall prophesy, your old men shall dream dreams, your young men shall see visions. Even upon the menservants and upon the handmaids in those days will I pour out My Spirit."

I see such a shortage of laborers for the Lord, especially among women. When I am speaking at a ladies' meeting and I ask how many want to be used by God, usually all hands are raised. But when I ask, "Okay, tomorrow let's meet here and I'll give you each an assignment for the Lord," and ask again for volunteers, the majority do not respond. Why? They are simply not prepared emotionally or spiritually. God wants to be your healer in all areas of your life -- spiritually, physically as well as emotionally. Most of us can believe God to heal a physical ailment, but when it comes to healing from the guilt of an abortion, the scars of divorce, or the trauma of sexual or physical abuse, we think, "No, this is what I have to live with." Many of you think this will always be a part of you. Satan wants to use your past to keep you from walking into your present freedom that God has provided. That is why Paul tells us in Philippians 3:13 to forget those things which are behind and reach forward to those things that are ahead. Also, Isaiah 43:18 tells us, "Remember ye not the former things, neither consider the things of old."

God has given me, along with other women as well as men, a mandate to help Him recruit women for His end-time army. He gave me a vision of three groups that were involved in becoming part of this end-time army.

The first group we will liken to a group of people trying to get into the United States Army. Some come unable to pass the physical because of past hurts and wounds and are denied entrance. Some Christians who would like to be used by God are also crippled by their pasts. Their eyes are on themselves instead of others and the Lord. These need to decide if they are going to carry those hurts and wounds or give them to Jesus who has already carried their rejection and paid the price. Isaiah 53:4(a) says, "Surely he hath borne our griefs, and carried our sorrows." When I was newly saved, I was in this group for a while. Many of you may be there too, but remember that you hold the key to moving on. Before I came to the Lord, I was physically, spiritually, and emotionally sick -- full of iniquity, rebellion, self-centeredness, hardness, low self-esteem, and much more. I could not help myself -- much less others --get out of a messed up life. Then I found Jesus, and because of what He did for me on Calvary, the healing process began.

At first I prayed and prayed, but only for my serious health problem to be healed. The Lord spoke to me and said that I first needed to be healed on the inside. Then my physical healing would manifest on the outside as well. You see, the body, soul, and spirit work together. All three parts of our personalities affect the others. Medical science has proven this to be true. Stress, fear, anger, or some other negative emotional reaction can literally make us sick or cause other negative symptoms in our bodies. As I gave God permission to do spiritual surgery on me, He gently and lovingly began to reveal things from my past that I needed to give to Him. Two important keys to emotional healings are:
1) receiving forgiveness from past mistakes and sins
2) forgiving others who have hurt you -- release and cancel their debt

Forgiveness is a gift given to those who don't deserve it! This is what Jesus did for us. Luke 17:1 in the King James Version tells us, "It is impossible but that offenses will come." People are not perfect, therefore, it is impossible to live in this world and not get hurt or disappoint one another.

My physical and emotional healing did not happen overnight. I had to receive God's forgiveness and remember that when He forgave my sin, He also forgot about it. It is Satan who likes to keep bringing it up. Another trick of the enemy is to make you think you are the only one that has ever had a particular negative thing happen to you. I taught the Women for the Harvest course at a Bible college for years, and it was not unusual for me to find out that over half of the class had been sexually or physically abused. So many of the girls told me that I was the first person they had ever told about what happened to them. You see, the darkness cannot be healed until it is exposed to the Light -- Jesus! There was comfort for them when I told them that they were not alone. Satan goes about as a roaring lion trying to hurt and destroy all of us -- not just you.

Our minds are like video recorders that play all the time. The tapes they are playing are called our life scripts; each of us receives our personal script from our parents, friends, teachers, husband, and other authority figures -- and it tells us who we "are." We listen to this message all our lives and eventually play out the role that it portrays to us. Proverbs 23:7 tells us that we become what we think in our hearts. In other words, what you believe or think about yourself is what you will act or live out. What you think about, you will talk about, and what you talk about, you will think about! I had a friend who was told all her life by her father that she was stupid, but that it was all right because she was beautiful. She said for years she believed this, and consequently performed poorly in school. She always thought her good looks were enough, like her daddy always told her. She then grew up and was saved and asked the Lord to change her negative self-esteem. As she went to church and Bible studies and began to meditate on and believe what the Word said about her (such as, "I have the mind of Christ," "I can do all things through Christ who strengthens me"), her self-image changed and she graduated not just high school, but college with honors. Proverbs 6:2 says, "You are snared with the words of your lips, you are caught by the speech of your mouth." (AMP) We say and do things without realizing that we are reinforcing our self-image for better or worse. Jesus wants to give us a new life script or self-image. He wants to tell you through His Word who you are. This is a major work that only the Holy Spirit can do as you yield to being changed. When you become His child, He wants to heal and break the bondages and yokes Satan has put on you. The people and circumstances that hurt you were certainly not from God.

Proverbs 18:14 says, "The strong spirit of a man sustains him in bodily pain or trouble, but a weak and broken spirit who can raise up or bear?" I once read a true story which shows us that a man can stand almost any attack on his body, but the thing that beats him is a broken heart. It is told that in the days of the Hitler terror that there was a man in Germany who was arrested, tried, tortured, and put into a concentration camp. He faced it all with gallantry and emerged erect and unbroken. Then by accident, he discovered who it was who had laid information against him -- it was his own son. The discovery broke him and he died. Attacks by an enemy he could bear; attacks by one whom he loved killed him.

As I let God show me the negative things in my life that were not only hurting me, but others, God started to manifest my physical healing. I also allowed Him to begin to deal with my rebellion. I asked Him to help me change and get rid of it and any other negative emotions I had. In the process, my physical healing was totally manifested.

Studies have shown that the number-one problem most women have is low self-esteem. Self-esteem is simply belief in yourself. The Bible tells us to love your neighbor as you love yourself. How can we manifest God's love toward others if we have not first allowed that love to operate toward our own selves?

Many of you need to ask God to change the way you think about yourself. If there are negative things that make you unkind or not as loveable or confident as you could be, ask God to show you what they are and begin the process of letting Him change and heal you. I could have stayed in my past by playing the blame game. Many women say to me, "You don't know what my parents did to me," or they tell me how traumatized they were in the past. Ladies, it is time to get up, get over, and get on with your new life in Christ. I know this sounds tough, but I work with and counsel women all the time and I have seen how these truths liberate them. It is when they come to this turning point in their thinking and decide that they are not going to let the devil have any more ground or victory in their lives that they step out and purposefully prove the devil wrong by doing something for the Lord. You need to choose -- are you going to listen to the father of lies (Satan) or your heavenly Father who created you for a reason and who has a perfect plan and purpose for your life? Someone once estimated that it takes seven positive thoughts to overcome every negative thing we hear about ourselves. We tend to latch onto the negative. That is why it is so important to read the Word and let it renew your mind. God does not want you to live in the image of anyone else other than Himself. Remember Paul who at first was called Saul and was a persecutor of Christians. Because God saw him differently, Paul became a great soul winner. Joseph, because he trusted God, went from being a prisoner to a prime minister. Mary Magdalene was delivered from seven demons and was chosen by God to be the first to announce His resurrection. Peter went from being a fisherman to an apostle who won three thousand converts in his first sermon. You need to realize that behind every rape, divorce, betrayal, rejection, and other painful event was the devil using a man or woman to hurt you. The devil, not a human individual, is your enemy. When you grasp this truth, you are on your way to being set free.

This brings me back to the vision the Lord showed me of His end-time army. As you get your eyes off yourself and onto the Lord and what His Word says, you become eligible as a candidate for group number two -- spiritual boot camp. This group is where He heals, changes, and develops those spiritual muscles, just as they do in the US Army boot camp. Here you are stripped, shaved, and made into a soldier who can defend herself and others from the enemy. Paul says in Philippians 1:21 that to die to yourself is gain. Again, God will not give you more than you can bear, but if you have some bad fruit in your life, I dare you to ask God why. He will get down to the root of why you are a certain way. Get counsel if you need it, and get into your prayer closet. Don't be the Great Pretender who never deals with the things in your life that are holding you back from being all you can be for Christ. His love never fails. You are His child. He hurts when you hurt and wants you to be healed and happy. Boot camp is your purification process that you will read about in the "Preparation Precedes Promotion" section of the next chapter. Though the Bible doesn't go into detail about the preparation that Esther had to go through to become queen, I am sure there were things she had to deal with -- things very similar to what you and I deal with in our own lives. Her parents died when she was young and she was left as an orphan. Talk about a trauma! If she hadn't been healed from this, she would not have been confident or bold enough to do all she had to do to save her people from being killed. She was willing to lay her life down and, consequently, the destiny that God had planned for her was fulfilled. Are you willing to pay the price to fulfill your destiny?

The last group I saw in the vision was group three -- those in active duty out on the field. Years ago, very few women were allowed in the army. Times have changed now, and we are slowly seeing women being given equal status with men -- both in the military and in the church. God wants us to be in His army and work along side the men. The women in group three had to go through process number one of passing the physical and process number two of going through spiritual boot camp to get healed and strengthened. The army officers know that you will not make it on the front line unless you have been prepared. Without proper preparation, you will be defeated or go AWOL. The same is true for us who want to serve the Lord -- you must be healed from your past or you will wind up being hurt, defeated, or destroyed by the people and situations you will have to deal with while serving Him. If your vessel is filled with insecurities, you will not be able to successfully help and heal others. You don't have to be perfect -- just healed and ready to be used. The woman whom God has set free will be able to fulfill the orders given by the Lord General and help others with the same healing they have received.

> Blessed be the God and Father of our Lord Jesus Christ, the Father of sympathy (pity and mercy) and the God [Who is the Source] of every comfort (consolation and encouragement), Who comforts (consoles and encourages) us in every trouble (calamity and affliction), so that we may also be able to comfort (console and encourage) those who are in any kind of trouble or distress, with the comfort (consolation and

encouragement) with which we ourselves are comforted (consoled and encouraged) by God. (II Corinthians 1:3-4, AMP)

What can you do to help the Lord set you free from your past?

1) Face your problem -- Acknowledge it to yourself and another person or persons.

2) Accept your responsibility -- Stop blaming everyone else and accept your part which is to let go of the problem and work with the Lord.

3) Ask yourself -- "Do I want to be healed or just keep talking about it?"

4) Forgive everyone involved -- "And whenever you stand praying, if you have anything against anyone, forgive him, that your Father in heaven may also forgive you your trespasses. But if you do not forgive, neither will your Father in heaven forgive your trespasses." (Mark 11:25-26)

5) Forgive yourself -- "There is therefore now no condemnation to those who are in Christ Jesus, who do not walk according to the flesh, but according to the Spirit." (Romans 8:1)

6) Ask the Holy Spirit what the real root of the problem is. God's love is the main factor in our emotional healing. That is why Satan is always trying to separate us from it! We are created for love -- to be loved and give love. If you can believe that God, who is perfect, loves you, then you can believe that you are worth loving! Once you begin to believe that you are accepted and loved by God, then you can begin accepting and loving yourself. Not only will you then start loving God in return, but you will also start loving others. Just start saying

over and over, "He loves me. He loves me. Jesus loves me!"

If you wonder why God doesn't deliver you from your bondages immediately, it is because He knows what needs to be done in the lives of His children as well as the perfect timing for it to be done. Have confidence in Jesus, and confidence in yourself. Then you will realize that the Christ in you is ever present to help you in all you need to do. John 15:5 tells you that, "Apart from Him you can do nothing." So when Satan tells you that you can't, you tell him back, "But the Jesus in me can!"

Let me share a story with you that will help to summarize the three groups in God's army. A young lady complained to her father about her life and how things had been so hard for her. She did not know how she was going to make it and she wanted to give up. She was tired of fighting and struggling. It seemed that just as soon as one problem was solved, another arose.

Her father, a chef, took her to the kitchen, filled three pots with water and placed them on the stove. Soon the three pots came to a boil. In one he placed carrots, in the other he placed eggs, and in the last pot he placed ground coffee beans. He let them sit and boil without saying a word. The daughter impatiently wondered what he was trying to do. She had problems, and he was making this strange concoction. In half an hour he walked over to the range and turned down the fire. He pulled the carrots out and placed them in a bowl. He pulled the eggs out and placed them in a bowl. Then he ladled the coffee out and placed the liquid in a bowl. Turning to her he asked, "Darling, what do you see?" Smartly, she replied, "Carrots, eggs, and coffee." He brought her closer and asked her to feel the carrots. She did and noted that they were soft. He then asked her to take an egg and break it. After pulling off the shell, she observed the hard-boiled egg. Finally, he asked her to sip the coffee. Her face frowned from the strength of the coffee. Humbly, she asked, "What does it mean, father?"

He explained. Each of them faced the same adversity, two hundred twelve degrees of boiling water. However, each reacted differently. The carrot went in strong, hard, and unrelenting, but after going through boiling water, it softened and became weak. The egg was fragile. A thin outer shell protected a liquid center, but after sitting through the boiling water, its inside became hardened. The coffee beans are unique, however. After they were in the boiling water, they became stronger and richer. "Which are you," he asked his daughter? "When adversity knocks on your door, how do you respond?" Are you a carrot, an egg, or a coffee bean? Are you the carrot that seems hard, but with the smallest amount of pain, adversity, or heat you wilt and become soft with no strength? Are you the egg, which starts off with a malleable heart and a fluid spirit, but after a death, a breakup, a divorce, or a layoff you become hardened and stiff? Your shell looks the same, but you are so bitter and tough, having a stiff spirit and heart, internally. Or are you like the coffee bean? The bean does not get its peak flavor until it reaches two hundred twelve degrees Fahrenheit. When the water gets the hottest, it just tastes better. When things are their worst, you get better.   When the hour is the darkest and trials are their greatest, your worship elevates to another level.   How do you handle adversity?   Are you a carrot, an egg, or a coffee bean?

The injured women in group one are hardened like the egg, needing a touch from God to get the healing process started.   The ladies who are being healed in group two are softened like the carrots and need to have their spiritual muscles strengthened so that they can better face adversity.   Those in the victorious group three are giving off the aroma of God like the coffee beans and are drawing many to Him.   Please don't let the broken things of yesterday spoil the good things and plans God has for you today.   Psalm 147:3 tells us that He heals the broken in heart and binds up their wounds!

There is a song by Sharon Daugherty titled, <u>You Can Start Over</u>.   When I have someone sing this at a meeting, I am always amazed at the reaction of tears and emotions that follows.   It simply says,

You can start over,
you can leave your past behind,
you can start over,
Jesus' blood can cleanse you inside.
He'll wash away all your sin
and help you start over again.
There once was a man named Peter,
He was one of the twelve,
who followed Jesus closely,
never dreaming that he might fail.
Yet three times he denied Him,
and what did Jesus say?
Tell Peter that I forgive him.
Have you failed and missed it?

Do you think no one cares?
Jesus never gives up on you
and He still hears your prayers.
He loves you and He believes in you.
He'll use your life if you believe
that the joys of the future
will swallow up
the "sorrows" of your past
and you'll be free!"
Jesus is the Master Mender.   Let Him heal you
so you can be the new creature in Christ He created
you to be.

Chapter Nine

PROMOTION COMES FROM THE LORD

I am often asked, "Where do I start?" Zechariah 4:10 tells us not to despise small beginnings. Start where there is a need. I did not start out at the pulpit in some large church, but in a small room packed with my son and other third-grade boys who needed a Sunday school teacher. It was hot and their greatest thrill was not to hear about my exciting Bible stories, but to see how many spit balls they could get to stick to the ceiling every time I looked down at my notes. When my children were very young, there were plenty of nursery and Sunday school opportunities for ministry. Because of my faithfulness in these small things, other doors opened.

Faithfulness is a key ingredient to being promoted by the Lord. His Word promises us in Matthew 25:23, "His master said to him, Well done, you upright (honorable, admirable) and faithful servant! You have been faithful and trustworthy over a little; I will put you in charge of much. Enter into and share the joy (the delight, the blessedness) which your master enjoys." I never missed a Sunday school class that I was assigned to have -- though I was tempted. I came in prepared, submitted, and kept my complaints to myself -- so began my next ministry after the nursery. From this, God gave me the desire to start a cell group. Actually, it was my friend and I who got permission from our pastor to start and organize the first cell groups at our church. With the Bible in one hand and a new baby in the other, I taught, prayed, and ministered to a group of women at my house. Sometimes I would spend hours cleaning and studying to have only one person show up, but I was faithful. Meanwhile, my husband, who was dean of the Bible college, was watching and listening to me when he came home for lunch while the meeting was going on. One day he unexpectedly said to me, "You're ready!" I said, "For what?" He replied, "The Bible college. I want you to develop and teach a class on what I have been hearing you teach here at our home here." Faithfulness to study, pray, and prepare had brought me to the next level of my ministry. From there, I went on to the mission field, prison ministry, and a myriad of other ministry opportunities.

God knows what He is doing when He makes plans for us and puts us in the middle of a ministry opportunity. Some of you drag behind God, holding back, convinced that you are not ready, educated, worthy, or confident enough. Remember, you are called and used by God not by your education, but by His impartation. I have sat and listened to people with a list of degrees, but with no anointing, and I didn't receive a thing.

Then there will be some of you who will run ahead of the Lord and unfortunately not be successful because you, not the Lord, pushed the door open. Let God bring your prophecies to pass; don't try to make them happen. Let Him direct your steps towards ministry. Proverbs 18:16 says, "A man's gift makes room for him, and brings him before great men." I once had a student in my Women for the Harvest class who had several prophecies about her future ministry. Basing her life on the prophecies rather than developing a daily walk with the Lord, she developed an unteachable spirit and began to think that she knew more than her teacher. The next thing I knew, she had sent out fancy invitations to a big ministry meeting she was going to have in an expensive hotel. I knew when I received mine that she was not ready and that this was her idea and not God's. As I expected -- no one showed up, and she was left with a large bill and a rather small ego.

Submission to authority is an absolute necessity to receive promotion in ministry, from man or the Lord. Hebrews 13:17 instructs us to "obey men that have the rule over you, and submit yourselves; for they watch for your souls, as they that must give account..." Before I got saved, I used to say, "I'll never submit to any man!" I was a true product of the ERA feminist movement and was determined not to let any man tell me what to do because that would mean that I was inferior and unequal. The first few years after I was born again, I tried to keep that attitude. As I read the Word and saw the divine order, I began to understand that everybody has to submit to the ones over them or there will be confusion and strife. For a Christian, submission really translates into a covering or protection for men as well as women; it does not mean that we are inferior or unequal to the person over us. Although it goes against our carnal nature not to do things our way, I have seen and learned the hard way that to be in authority, you have to submit to authority.

Many times I don't always enjoy submitting to my husband -- but when I do, God is always pleased. I discover that there is a good reason I was asked to do something that I might not have agreed upon. To be under authority is God's way of protecting us from ourselves. We can get off balance, puffed up, and emotional. How many ministers of the gospel do you know who have fallen because they weren't accountable and submissive to someone?

I am convinced that the reason I was given the position over the women's ministry at our last church was because I submitted and showed a teachable spirit through my years of performing any type of service at the church. For example, I was asked, along with another lady, to come up to the pulpit and share something with the congregation. We were told, "No more than two minutes each." I took one minute and sat down. The other person went over the two minutes and had no intention of stopping until the pastor actually had to take the microphone away from her -- much to her embarrassment. It was her own fault that she was never again allowed to speak, whereas I was allowed to share on a regular basis. You may not always agree or see why you are asked to do something, but do it anyway unless it is against what you know is morally or ethically correct.

Some of you are going to have to wait on the Lord for things He has prepared for you. Before I received my official chaplain's badge for the county jail, it took months of prayer and red tape. But I know that this is what God wanted me to do at this season of my life. You will also have seasonal changes. Some doors to minister will seem to take so long to come to pass -- like waiting for spring through a long dreary winter. But don't give up -- just wait on the Lord.

Only God can put you where He wants you to be in His timing. For many years, the women at our last church were not allowed to do altar ministry with their husbands. Only the male elders and pastors were allowed. Many Sundays I just yearned and burned to be up there with my husband, who was an associate pastor. The Lord told me just to pray and that one day it would be time to go to the pastor for permission for the women to be allowed at the altar with the men. Finally, my wait was over. It's like I heard the Lord say, "Green light -- go." So I humbly and carefully approached the pastor. After what seemed like years of waiting, it was over in just a few minutes as he granted the women permission. I'll never forget his looking at me like, "What's the problem?" Then he said, "If one can chase a thousand, two can chase ten thousand." The next Sunday was a real thrill, break through, and step forward for the pastors' and elders' wives. We were finally able to join our husbands at the altar to pray with the congregation after years of having to sit in the pews. The passage in I Peter 5:6 has certainly proved to be true for my life, "Therefore humble yourselves [demote, lower yourselves in your own estimation] under the mighty hand of God, that in due time He may exalt you." (AMP)

Another one of the highlights in my ministry concerning promotion came right before we left our church after twenty-five years of service. As director of the women's ministries, I had received permission for many women to be guest speakers.

Some were invited for our women's meetings and some came to speak for our entire church. One day the Lord spoke to me, "As you have promoted and placed many women in the pulpit, you will now be promoted and asked to speak to the entire church." It was one thing, I thought, for our pastor to allow people such as Gloria Copeland to speak, but to ask a woman from our congregation to take a service was surely a first. I never asked for the privilege, but I was eventually invited to speak at a Sunday night service. Why? Because I had been faithful and submitted, and because I let God promote me. I was greeted with a standing ovation when I went up to the pulpit. Not because of me, Peggy Shirley. Heavens no! It was because it was a breakthrough for the women to at last be recognized as vessels that God could speak through. What a service we had that night, thanks to the Lord!

Preparation Precedes Promotion

God is looking for prepared, not perfect vessels. As I studied the book of Esther, I was amazed to see how God took an ordinary woman with an orphan background and turned her into a queen. Why? Because she had a destiny -- a plan to fulfill which only she could bring to pass as God had predestined. The same is true for you who are reading these lessons. God had a reason for creating you -- an assignment that He has picked for you and you alone to do. How exciting! I would have never dreamed, as a rebellious teenager, that one day the Lord would be using me to minister to others. I'm sure that Esther never dreamed that she had an assignment to save her people from being annihilated.

Esther was raised by her cousin Mordecai since she had no family. As did Esther, you need to leave your past, no matter how tragic or dysfunctional. You need to focus on your future and not your past. God could have used Mordecai or some other man of importance to influence the king not to kill the Jews, but I believe He intentionally chose a Jewish woman who would go down in history. King Ahasuerus needed a queen to replace the former queen, Vashti, whom he had banished because of her lack of submission towards him. The choosing of a new queen was a long process. Each woman had to submit to twelve months of purification even before the king set eyes on her! For Esther, who believed in the Lord, this was a spiritual as well as a physical time of purifying and getting ready. Many people may shake mountains with their credentials and build kingdoms with their skills, but in the end, what will count for eternity will not be what is accomplished with our abilities, but what God accomplished through our faith and obedience.

God will never force you to do anything. For the first few years of being saved, I resisted the call on my life because of fear and false teaching against women. My husband is the one who saw my call to the ministry, and like Mordecai, encouraged me and prayed for me to fulfill it. But ultimately, I had to say, "Yes, Lord, if You can use anybody, Lord, then here I am."

To purify means to make pure and to free from anything that pollutes or contaminates. It is not always an easy process. As the king needed a queen with a pure heart who would submit to him, so does the Lord. Many of us have things from our past, such as rebellion, in our lives that would hinder -- if not destroy -- our work for the Lord. I have seen jealousy, competition, pride, and other elements of the world that polluted people in ministry. Why? Because they didn't allow God to break them and make them into what they needed to be to serve Him successfully. Purification is a process that will always be a part of our lives as we strive to be more like Him. But God needs us to take off our masks and be real with Him and ask Him to take out the pollution.

Be a woman of prayer, fasting, and brokenness. As a result of Esther's submitting and cleansing, she was chosen above a host of other candidates wanting to be the next queen. Esther 2:17 records, "And the king loved Esther more than all the women, and she obtained grace and favor in his sight more than all the maidens, so that he set the royal crown on her head and made her queen instead of Vashti." (AMP)

Remember that King Ahasuerus made her queen. She didn't beg or push herself into this position. Men do not like pushy, forceful, brassy women. Stay humble. Ask God for holy boldness so that all will see that your promotion is from God. Make suggestions, then pray, if your leaders do not agree with you about things you would like to do in ministry or at your church. Take it to the Lord. In the past, when I was in charge of the women's ministry at our church, I had arranged a special speaker for one of our women's meetings.

Everyone was so excited as we had waited a long time to get an opening in her schedule to come speak to us. One day I got a call from the pastor's secretary, telling us that the pastor had changed his mind and that we would have to cancel the meeting. I was so disappointed as I knew the ladies would be, but more importantly, I sensed that the Lord was grieved. I fasted and prayed as Esther did before she had to go before the king. She too had to change the king's mind about killing her people. My husband told me that it was a waste of time to try to convince the pastor to change his mind. He told me, "Once he said no, it meant no." I knew that I had to be obedient to what God had told me to do. As I stepped out in faith and obedience and had a meeting with the pastor, God honored me. God had gone before me, and -- to my husband's surprise -- the pastor gave me permission once again to have her. That meeting opened the doors for other women ministers to speak from the pulpit at our church and was God ordained.

Esther helped save her people because she heard from the Lord due to her close relationship with Him. It was the same for me. I dared to challenge and change my pastor's decision because I heard from the Lord due to my close walk with Him. Your ministry or service to the Lord depends upon this. Keep a total reliance on Him. As we become more confident, we tend to become more self-reliant and less God-reliant.

All of you women have divine destinies. You need to get into your spirit, as God told Esther through her cousin Mordecai in Esther 4:14, "For if you keep silent at this time, relief and deliverance shall arise for the Jews from elsewhere, but you and your father's house will perish. And who knows but that you have come to the kingdom for such a time as this and for this very occasion?" (AMP) We all have people, places, and things waiting for us -- assigned only to us and us alone. Several years ago, I was on a missionary trip to Africa. I never dreamed, as I was pulling into the house that we were staying at, that God had a special assignment just for me. I was surrounded by men, and my husband was at my side, but He had me in mind to do His will. The house we were staying at just happened to belong to the ambassador of the country of Rwanda, who was not saved. As we interacted with him while we stayed in his home he watched and listened. I had no idea what the Lord was doing. The last night a group of all male leaders and pastors came over to thank us for our time of ministry to them. All of a sudden, in the middle of our conversation, the ambassador stood up, looked and pointed to me, and said, "I want what you have, Peggy." And I, as the Lord's ambassador, had the privilege of leading the ambassador of Rwanda to the Lord. Why me? Why not one of the Rwandan pastors or my husband who stayed in his house with me? Why? Because I was called for such a time. God is no respecter of persons. You, too, have your "Esther" or "Peggy" assignments. Oh, it is so exciting working together with the Lord!

How long your preparation lasts is up to the Lord. He may start letting you witness, lay on hands on people, or do other things for Him right away after you are born again. I had just gotten saved when I led my homosexual hairdresser to the Lord. I hardly knew what to do. But as you grow in the Lord and are faithful with a little, He will give you more. As you surrender, submit your will to His, humble yourself, and give Him permission to change, heal, teach, and impart, you will find that this is the key to unlocking even more and new doors. I could have never done the prison ministry He has called me to when I was in the first years of ministry. But, He has put much in me through my lessons along the way with Him, and now I am prepared and ministering with great results. The glory be to God!

How serious are you about serving the Lord? Purging and purifying by the Lord takes a dying to yourself so that He might shine forth. This time is not always easy or without a price to pay, but, the end result is so worth it all! Remember, God uses us in spite of ourselves. He alone is perfect. All you have to do is to allow Him to start the process.

What About My Family?

The first priority is to your family when choosing ways to serve in any type of ministry. There must be a balance in what you do for the Lord. Obviously, those with younger children will not be able to be as involved or do things like the women whose children are older or like those who are empty nesters.

But don't let your children stop you. God knows you need to serve Him as well as your family. When I had my three boys, there were months where I did nothing but nurse, burp, and bathe. But as I was able to leave them for meetings, shopping, etc., I began to get active again in ministry. The Lord told me to develop a course to teach women to be a part of the end-time harvest. As I had gone through a process and finally was set free to be all that God created me to be, He wanted me to teach all that I had been taught and to mentor others to step out into ministry. So I wrote material for Women for the Harvest while my three sons were still young. When my last son was born and the other two were in school, I went to our Bible college library and spent hours studying and developing the material for this course. My baby slept and stayed with the babysitter and was quite content. I always watched my time as I wrote, and I saw God stretch my time to complete this course in months.

Always let the head of your house, your husband, give you his blessing on what you want to do for the Lord. He can see the overall picture as well as your heart and help you to decide what you should or should not do. One of my motivational gifts is that of a server. I was always saying yes to the needs I saw in the Body. One night my husband said, "Peggy, I am tired of your leftovers." I thought he was talking about dinner, to which I said, "Well, tonight I prepared everything fresh." He said, "I am not talking about your food leftovers, but your time and energy." He then proceeded to tell me how I was putting others before the family because of my servant's heart, and that the family was getting my leftovers. From then on I asked him before I jumped in on a project, ministry meeting, or whatever else seemed to need me. If your husband doesn't support your decision to do whatever you are called to do, there will be resentment -- especially if you have kids and you leave him and run off. He also knows better than you what you can handle to keep that balance of mother and minister.

So all of this is saying that you young mothers do not have to wait until your children are raised to do ministry. The Lord clearly told me I didn't have time to wait until my house was empty, but as I trusted Him, He would make a way. Sometimes I had a Bible in one hand teaching from it and a baby in the other, but somehow I always managed. One day when I was feeling sorry for myself, I asked the Lord, "Isn't motherhood enough of a ministry?" Later that day I just happened to read an article by Marilyn Hickey telling how the Lord told her to start her television ministry when her children were only three and eleven years old. I quickly remembered that in my weakness, He would be my strength, and He was and always has been. Even when my boys were young, I did mission trips. At first I resisted because somehow the devil convinced me that my children would die or be forever traumatized if I left them for a few weeks, but the opposite was true. They always told me about the fun they had with their babysitters, who for many years were my in-laws. Because I chose to obey, many lives -- as well as my own -- were forever touched by the Lord. We even took all three boys on some of the trips -- now, that was a challenge! We didn't do it often, but as a result, two out of my three children want to go on mission trips now that they are grown.

Lydia, in Acts chapter sixteen, had a part-time ministry, whereas Deborah, in Judges chapter four, was in full-time ministry as a judge. God knows the seasons of your lives.   Serving Him while your children are young is a challenge, but He can more than help you meet that challenge.   As you have more free time and fewer responsibilities at home, He will give you more opportunities to serve Him.

James Dobson of Focus on the Family says, "The most important job a woman will ever have is that of being a mother."   As mothers, we have a tremendous influence on our children.   One of your greatest accomplishments will be passing the faith inside of you on to your children.   If there is anything this country needs today, it is more godly mothers.   Charles Spurgeon, one of the greatest preachers of all times, said, "I can tell you two reasons why I am what I am -- my mother and the truth of my message."   Martin Luther wrote about his mother, "Much of the blessing of my life was due to the influence of my mother."   Former president of the United States, Abraham Lincoln, said, "All that I am or hope to be, I owe to my angel mother." There will always be people who need your touch, prayers, and whatever gift or talent God has given you.   Just remember -- your family must come first.

Chapter Ten

THE "DO"s AND "DON'T"s OF MINISTRY

When people think of ministry, they almost always think of someone in one of the five-fold ministries. Many of you reading this are destined to be -- or may already be involved in one of these offices; however, there will be many of you doing other things which are just as valuable to the Body and to the Lord. The Hebrew word for ministry is *sharath*. It means: (1) to contribute to, (2) to serve, (3) to wait on, (4) to attend to people's spiritual needs, (5) to minister to God by serving His people. Therefore, ministry is any service done for God.

Although I have been in the ministry for over thirty years now, I will be the first to admit that I still have much to learn. As you get older, the knowledge you glean is surpassed by wisdom which is far more valuable. This wisdom comes from life experiences and watching others make it in the ministry. Over the years, I've seen churches split and ministries fall as well as ministers and ministries start from nothing and become powerful successes. In addition to my own personal experiences, I have gained some deep insights into situations which -- although I personally didn't experience all of them -- I felt their impact as I walked with others whom I was counseled by as they were going through them. In my spiritual journey, I have made lots of choices -- some good and some not so good -- but all of them have taught me principles I would like to pass on. They are simple, yet so vital, to anyone trying to serve the Lord. Do read and study these principles; if you try to apply these truths you will save yourself a lot of sorrow and mistakes.

Do know that you were created by God to give Him pleasure! "For the Lord takes pleasure in His people." (Psalms 149:4) I always tell people that they were born with two empty vacuums. One of these vacuums needs to be filled by being born again and allowing Jesus to come into your life. The second vacuum is to be filled by serving the Lord. God created us this way. Truly fulfilled people not only have Christ as their Lord and Savior, but are doing something for others. Happy living is rooted in giving. It is so pleasing to God when you choose to follow His example in the Bible of being a servant, actively choosing to serve the Body as He did. "You have not chosen me, but I have chosen you that you should go and bring forth fruit and that your fruit should remain." (John 15:16)

For the first years that I was saved, I used the excuse that I had children and that was the only ministry I needed. I sat in the pew comfortably watching my husband teach and minister. The nursery duty I had was all I needed. But the Lord began to deal with me. He told me that I was not going to be able to claim my husband's achievements at my final judgment and that He had work waiting for me. I said, "Ok -- only after the children are raised." He spoke again and said that I did not have the time to wait until they were grown up. He needed me now, and I could do both with His help and grace.

Do remember that you were created uniquely, so there is no need to compare your gifts and talents to others. Matthew 25, which we discussed earlier clearly makes it known that some will have more talents and, therefore, more responsibilities than others. The only thing that mattered to Jesus at the end of the parable was that each servant had done something with the talent(s) he was given. I have seen so many people look at the big evangelists, teachers, missionaries, etc., and think that if they weren't having large meetings or ministering in foreign countries as these people were, then what they were doing wasn't that important. As Mother Teresa once said, "We ourselves feel that what we are doing is just a drop in the ocean, but the ocean would be less because of that missing drop."

Do know that when you serve the Lord in whatever way He has called you, there is much joy and fulfillment. I have traveled all over the world, lived in a foreign country, ridden elephants and camels, experienced much of the good life, but nothing can compare to what I feel after I have done something for the Lord. When we first moved to Colorado, I had to leave my ministry in Indiana with all the lists of things I was involved in for the Lord. That all stopped when we moved. At first, it was a nice break -- but not for long. I can't describe the longing and emptiness in my life when I wasn't able to be in active ministry. I felt I had no purpose. Finally, after many months, I was accepted as a chaplain at the county jail. When I returned home after my first meeting there, I was on Cloud Nine.

As I was telling my family about the hardened felons crying and accepting Christ, I was dancing and singing, "This is what I was born for!" Those of you who have assignments from the Lord and are able to see the fruit of your labor know exactly what I am talking about. The rest of you have much fulfillment and purpose awaiting as you get involved in doing things for the Lord.

Do expect signs and wonders to follow if you believe. When I go out on the mission field or to the jail, I pray and go believing for salvations, healings, deliverances, and whatever else the Lord wants to happen. If I look with carnal eyes when the girls come into my meetings at the jail, I would turn around and probably walk out. Many of them are hard and cold and come in with an attitude. Some even have a mocking spirit. But I just tell the Lord, "This is Your meeting; You are in charge; let Your presence come," and He has not failed me. It is so exciting to see what the Lord will do through you when you allow Him to flow in and through you. Mark 16:15-20 says that the disciples went out and preached and the Lord worked with them with signs and wonders.

Do be quick to give Him all the glory. The Lord told Aimee Semple McPherson, "If at anytime people try to call you the 'Miracle Woman' and try to say that you healed them, you will have no power. Whatever the results are, you are to say, 'The glory belongs to the Lord.'" But this was not just a mandate for her; it a universal truth taught in Luke 18:4, "For everyone who exalts himself shall be humbled, but he who humbles himself shall be exalted." It will be tempting to think, "Did I do that?" after you see someone saved, healed, or delivered, but if it wasn't for the anointing from Jesus, the Anointed One, your words and actions would produce no results.

Do remember to never get too busy for time away with the Lord. This time alone is where your strength lies. The enemy knows this truth and will try to keep you from this private time with God. You must come apart with the Lord, or else you will come apart physically, emotionally, and spiritually. Coming into His presence through praising, praying, and reading His Word is how we build ourselves up so that we can go back out to do what He has called us to do. During this private time, God will give you correction if it is needed. This quiet time is also when He will give you direction or encouragement or just talk to you. As Dick Eastman said, "Prayer is not optional. On the contrary, it is obligatory. Where there is an absence of prayer, there will be an absence of power. Where there is a frequency of prayer, there will be a continuing display of God's power." Jesus was our example in Mark 1:35, "And in the morning, rising up a great while before day, he went out, and departed into a solitary place, and there prayed."

Do remember the power and anointing you were given when you received the baptism of the Holy Spirit. People who are not Spirit-filled do not have this same power. Even though Peter followed Jesus throughout His ministry, he denied the Lord three times before His crucifixion because he was afraid. However, after he was filled with the Holy Spirit, this same Peter did bold things for the Lord, and faith -- instead of fear -- filled him. We need to remember this as Christian women. We do not have to work up, or fast, or beg for some special anointing. It is already ours. While it is good to pray, fast, and prepare yourself for ministry, the anointing is not something you have to strive to attain. It took me a while in ministry to realize this. I thought that I had to lock myself away, fast, and get all ready before God would bring the power down.

One night I had been asked to supervise the chapel services at the Bible college where my husband was dean. However, I had one last task to complete at home before I headed out to the school -- to bathe my dear four-year-old son. Well, on this particular night, he thought that it would be fun to baptize Mommy as I was stooped over the bathtub. Without warning, he turned on the shower and soaked me. I was already running late -- as was the babysitter, so I quickly went and changed and rushed off to the campus. As I sat in the back of the chapel with my hair looking like a wet mop, the only place I wanted to be was home. Just as the meeting was over, the Lord spoke to me to go up and minister to the students as a conclusion to the meeting. When the student who had preached sat down, I was obedient -- though it was the last thing I wanted to do. Out of my obedience, the anointing flowed through me, wet mop and all. Very few students were left standing as I laid hands on them. The presence of God was so strong that I could barely stand. After it was over, I just sat there as the students went on to their evening class. I asked the Lord how He could have possibly used me, considering my mood and lack of preparation. It was a simple reply -- He said that He moved because there were students who needed to be set free. Because of my obedience and trust, His power was able to flow through me. He showed me clearly that His anointing was not something I earned or had to work for.

The anointing is ours to use at any time. "And you shall receive power, after that the Holy Ghost has come upon you." (Acts 1:8) "And when they had entered, they went up to the upper room...They were all with one mind continually devoting themselves to prayer, along with the women..." (Acts 1:13-14) Why would Jesus allow the women to be baptized with the Holy Ghost and power and then not be able to go out and use it? As we have seen in a previous chapter, He did allow the women to minister and Paul commended them because they co-labored with him. "And it shall come to pass in the last days, saith God, I will pour out my Spirit upon all flesh and your sons and your daughters shall prophesy and your young men shall see visions and your old men shall dream dreams. And on my servants and on my handmaidens I will pour out in those days of my Spirit, and they shall prophesy." (Acts 2:17) Jesus said He would pour out -- not just send a few drops -- His Spirit upon His daughters and handmaidens. If you don't have this power, you need to ask the Lord to baptize you in the Holy Ghost. It's easy to receive and is just another free gift that He wants to give you -- like the gift of salvation.

<u>Don't</u> have <u>jealousy</u> <u>towards</u> <u>others</u>. On the other hand, don't be surprised when you learn that other Christian ministers are jealous of you. Satan knows that, "Where there is envy and strife, there is every evil thing." (James 3:16) Since you are on the front lines of God's army when you start doing things for the Lord's Kingdom, he will try to disqualify, discourage, or disable you one way or another -- either through you being jealous of others or by being discouraged when others become jealous of you. My late pastor, Dr. Lester Sumrall, who worked in the ministry from age seventeen until his home-going at eighty-three years of age, told me, "The more you do for the Lord, the more you will get hurt. It comes with the territory. The Bible tells us, 'Woe to you when everyone speaks well of you...'" (Luke 6:26)

<u>Don't</u> <u>accept</u> <u>bitterness</u> <u>and</u> <u>unforgiveness</u>. Guard yourself against offenses. "It is impossible but that offences will come: but woe unto him, through whom they come!" (Luke 17:1) We must walk in Christ's *agape* love and forgiveness and understand that to hold on to an offense is to fall right into Satan's plan. Some of our greatest hurts and disappointments will be from other Christians. Why? Because we expect more from them.

<u>Don't</u> <u>forget</u> <u>that</u> <u>you</u> <u>are</u> <u>a</u> <u>lady</u> -- <u>act</u> <u>like</u> <u>one</u>. Keep your shoes on! Wear comfortable shoes so you won't have to take them off. I have seen women ministers kick off their shoes in a number of

meetings. Everybody in the audience noticed what these women had done, and -- honestly -- it was very unprofessional and greatly distracted from their ministry. Dress appropriately. Tops or dresses should not be too short or too tight. Be modest. Some of the men watching you will easily be distracted by clothing that draws attention to your body. Don't feel like you have to shout or be loud to be noticed. It is the anointing that will get people's attention. Be feminine just as God created you to be -- not pushy and brassy. You don't have to prove yourself. Relax and let God do the work.

Don't ever fail to submit to the people you are ministering for. Be careful not to go over the time they give you to speak or violate whatever rules you are given. At the jail where I serve as a chaplain, I have pages of rules which I must submit to. At first, I just wanted to resign because there were so many. How could God possibly flow through me when I felt like a prisoner? But God honors obedience, and I soon saw God can work and flow even in the strictest of places or conditions.

Don't forget to keep a servant's heart at all times no matter what position or ministry He puts you into. Over the years I have had the opportunity to work with many of the nation's top speakers, and I can tell you that I've seen it all! Some arrived with their entourage as if they were movie stars. They were unapproachable and you would have had a hard time believing that they had come for the purpose of ministering to the Body. Others were humble and friendly. It was obvious that they were there to serve the Body. They were there for one reason -- to show the love of Jesus and to emulate His ministry of being a servant. Jesus was our perfect example. He came to serve and not be served. Remember, whatever you do unto the least of them, you do it unto the Lord. (Matthew 25:40)

Don't let compromise or a lack of integrity into your ministry. There will be temptations, but stay sensitive to your conscience. Always have people watching over you so that you are accountable to those who will correct, counsel, and guide you into what is right. This purposeful protection will keep you from falling or getting into error.

Don't let pride come in. Since pride was the reason for Lucifer's downfall, he is keenly aware that we are all susceptible to pride and that it can be a powerful tool in destroying us and our ministries. Therefore, it is one of his favorite tricks to get you off track. A modern proverb warns, "Praise is like perfume. It's okay to smell it as long as you don't swallow it." Likewise an ancient Proverb bluntly states, "Pride goes before destruction and a haughty spirit before stumbling." (Proverbs 16:18, AMP) Just as we mentioned before, this is another area where you need to have people around you who will speak into your life to warn you if you are beginning to fall for the devil's tricks. These people need to be individuals with wisdom and experience, not just people who think you are great and that you can do no wrong. They must be objective and be brave enough to correct you if they see pride creeping in or sense that you are making a wrong decision.

CONCLUSION

Before I was born again, I spent over a month in the hospital struggling with an incurable disease and the suicidal depression that accompanied it. Then someone -- someone just like you -- came into my room and witnessed to me about the love of Jesus. Because of this stranger's divine appointment, I was saved from suicide and hell. Until that visit, I had spent my life searching for meaning, and -- even though I had a good career and had traveled around the world -- I had no clue where to find the truth that I so desperately needed. Instead of the devil ending my life, I surrendered it to Christ and found the real beginning of life. Now, just as the Lord had an assignment for the person who came to me in the hospital, I have determined to fulfill my divine assignment by stepping into others' lives to bring them the good news that will save and set them free. Plus, I am on another level of that assignment -- awakening other women to the fact that they, too, have divine assignments in life. Today I am able to use the personal experiences I have gone through and the understanding that I have gained from those experiences to write this book as a help to you. Thus, the chain reaction from Christ goes on.

Second Corinthians 1:4 says, "Who comforteth us in all our tribulation, that we may be able to comfort them which are in any trouble, by the comfort wherewith we ourselves are comforted of God." That's what I pray has happened as you have read these pages -- that the encouragement that the Lord brought into my life has also filtered into yours.

Many of us are sensing that something powerful is on the horizon for the workers in the Body of Christ. On one hand we see Satan pouring out all his deception, lies, and immorality; however, on the other hand there are also many prophecies from God's generals that there is going to be one final wave of the Holy Ghost with powerful signs and wonders that we have yet to experience. Just listen to how Steve Hill, who led a world renowned revival in Brownsville, Florida, expressed his vision:

> In the months and years ahead, God's people are going to become acutely aware of the spiritually malnourished around them. He will reveal to us the depth of their cravings as if we were watching a documentary on starvation. The spiritually sensitive are going to experience revelation knowledge of those who are dying of spiritual mal nutrition and disease. Vivid images of their desperate plight will be dropped into our spirits. This will take place in schools, shopping malls, the local grocery store -- anywhere we find the spiritually destitute. There will be "divine appointments" that reach into the lives of people who often know nothing of biblical principles and doctrines. All they know is that some brave heart just read their mail.

One thing we know about this final outpouring is

that only those who are "tuned in" and "turned on" to the Holy Ghost will be able to be part of it. If you will allow Him to have full control of your life, the Holy Spirit will take away any fear that is holding you in bondage and replace it with a boldness that you have never had before.

Proverbs 18:16 says that your gift will make room for you and bring you before great men. You may say, "But I don't know where to start or where to go." Just lay your life down. Give Him permission to send you wherever He wants you to go and to assign you to whatever task He wants you to do. Some of you will be going places and doing things for the Lord you have never dreamed of or thought would be possible. Don't let Satan use your problems or imperfections to stop you. We, as women, need to press beyond our fears and lack of confidence. We read how even Aimee, Kathryn, and Mother Teresa felt that they could do nothing without Him. They, too, had to face their fears. Always remember what He told Aimee.

> You tell the people what I am going to do, and when you lay your hands on them, I will lay My hand on yours and all the time you are standing there, I will be standing right back of you. And when you speak the Word, I will send the power of the Holy Ghost. You are simply the mouthpiece of the telephone. You are the key on the typewriter. You are only a mouth through which the Holy Ghost can speak. Will you go now?

When you start to think or say as Moses did, "Who am I that I should go?" the Lord will answer you as He did to Moses, "I will be with you." T. L. Osborne once said, "As we lift people, we are lifted. In healing people, we are healed. In loving people, we are loved. In serving people, we are truly serving our Lord." Ephesians 2:10 tells us that we were created to do good works. Yet many women have never been encouraged in their callings or given the truths that I have shared with you in this book. The tragic result is that many women have felt incomplete as Christians simply because they haven't been fulfilling the purpose and call upon their lives to serve Him with these good works.

Ladies, there are people waiting for you -- you women for the harvest. Let's go to them -- one precious soul at a time. And as we go, we will leave a legacy -- a legacy of unapologetic love and service to the Lord.